Dedicated to Albert Harrison Small

esteemed alumnus of the University of Virginia

with deep gratitude for his lifelong devotion
to collecting and preserving our national heritage

and for the extraordinary gift of his renowned collection
on the Declaration of Independence and its signers
to the University of Virginia

so that the world may be informed and inspired
by this pivotal time in our nation's history.

DECLARING INDEPENDENCE

The Origin and Influence of America's Founding Document

PREFACE

David McCullough

ESSAYS

David Armitage, Pauline Maier,
Robert M.S. McDonald, and Robert G. Parkinson

EPILOGUE

Justice Sandra Day O'Connor

Christian Y. Dupont and Peter S. Onuf

Editors

Featuring the

ALBERT H. SMALL DECLARATION OF INDEPENDENCE COLLECTION

University of Virginia Library
Charlottesville, Virginia
2008

Library of Congress Control Number: 2007908142
ISBN: 978-0-9799997-0-3

The paper used in this book conforms to ANSI/NISO Z39.48-1992 (R2002) standard for Permanence of Paper for Publications and Documents in Libraries and Archives.

Printed by Progress Printing, Lynchburg, Virginia

Designed by Gibson Design Associates

Contents

Preface

*A*S HAS BEEN AMPLY DOCUMENTED DOWN THE YEARS, but tends at times to be overlooked, those we call the founders of the nation were neither supermen nor gods. They were, without exception, perfectly capable of being mistaken, inconsistent, contradictory, vain, selfish, at times self-deceiving, at times dead-wrong—quite as much as the rest of us. History makes the point again and again. Thomas Jefferson made the point in the very first words of the first line of the Declaration of Independence. "When in the course of human events ..." Read aloud, the accent should be on *human*.

But evidence of our humanity is not to be found in our failings alone, as history also makes abundantly clear, and as those same courageous notables who gave language and resolve to the American Revolution demonstrated with such far-reaching effect.

What is so magnificent, and ought always to command our respect as well as understanding, is that those same mere mortals, under the most trying circumstances and with no guarantee of success, could rise to achieve all that they did. And there are few more stirring examples of their noble attainments than the Declaration of Independence.

The Declaration of Independence is a statement of conviction and intent. When Jefferson wrote that "all men are created equal," he, a slave master, knew perfectly how much had still to be done by those who would follow to attain such a society in fact not theory. But that is part of our strength, that we Americans are called on, one generation after another, to achieve the promise. We have a star to steer by.

— *David McCullough*

IN CONGRESS, JULY 4, 1776.

A DECLARATION

BY THE REPRESENTATIVES OF THE

UNITED STATES OF AMERICA,

IN GENERAL CONGRESS ASSEMBLED.

WHEN in the Course of human Events, it becomes neceffary for one People to diffolve the Political Bands which have connected them with another, and to affume among the Powers of the Earth, the feparate and equal Station to which the Laws of Nature and of Nature's God entitle them, a decent Refpect to the Opinions of Mankind requires that they fhould declare the caufes which impel them to the Separation.

WE hold thefe Truths to be felf-evident, that all Men are created equal, that they are endowed by their Creator with certain unalienable Rights, that among thefe are Life, Liberty, and the Purfuit of Happinefs---That to fecure thefe Rights, Governments are inftituted among Men, deriving their juft Powers from the Confent of the Governed, that whenever any Form of Government becomes deftructive of thefe Ends, it is the Right of the People to alter or to abolifh it, and to inftitute new Government, laying its Foundation on fuch Principles, and organizing its Powers in fuch Form, as to them fhall feem moft likely to effect their Safety and Happinefs. Prudence, indeed, will dictate that Governments long eftablifhed fhould not be changed for light and tranfient Caufes; and accordingly all Experience hath fhewn, that Mankind are more difpofed to fuffer, while Evils are fufferable, than to right themfelves by abolifhing the Forms to which they are accuftomed. But when a long Train of Abufes and Ufurpations, purfuing invariably the fame Object, evinces a Defign to reduce them under abfolute Defpotifm, it is their Right, it is their Duty, to throw off fuch Government, and to provide new Guards for their future Security. Such has been the patient Sufferance of thefe Colonies; and fuch is now the Neceffity which conftrains them to alter their former Syftems of Government. The Hiftory of the prefent King of Great-Britain is a Hiftory of repeated Injuries and Ufurpations, all having in direct Object the Eftablifhment of an abfolute Tyranny over thefe States. To prove this, let Facts be fubmitted to a candid World.

HE has refufed his Affent to Laws, the moft wholefome and neceffary for the public Good.

HE has forbidden his Governors to pafs Laws of immediate and preffing Importance, unlefs fufpended in their Operation till his Affent fhould be obtained; and when fo fufpended, he has utterly neglected to attend to them.

HE has refufed to pafs other Laws for the Accommodation of large Diftricts of People, unlefs thofe People would relinquifh the Right of Reprefentation in the Legiflature, a Right ineftimable to them, and formidable to Tyrants only.

HE has called together Legiflative Bodies at Places unufual, uncomfortable, and diftant from the Depofitory of their public Records, for the fole Purpofe of fatiguing them into Compliance with his Meafures.

HE has diffolved Reprefentative Houfes repeatedly, for oppofing with manly Firmnefs his Invafions on the Rights of the People.

HE has refufed for a long Time, after fuch Diffolutions, to caufe others to be elected; whereby the Legiflative Powers, incapable of Annihilation, have returned to the People at large for their exercife; the State remaining in the mean time expofed to all the Dangers of Invafion from without, and Convulfions within.

HE has endeavoured to prevent the Population of thefe States; for that Purpofe obftructing the Laws for Naturalization of Foreigners; refufing to pafs others to encourage their Migrations hither, and raifing the Conditions of new Appropriations of Lands.

HE has obftructed the Adminiftration of Juftice, by refufing his Affent to Laws for eftablifhing Judiciary Powers.

HE has made Judges dependent on his Will alone, for the Tenure of their Offices, and the Amount and Payment of their Salaries.

HE has erected a Multitude of new Offices, and fent hither Swarms of Officers to harrafs our People, and eat out their Subftance.

HE has kept among us, in Times of Peace, Standing Armies, without the confent of our Legiflatures.

HE has affected to render the Military independent of and fuperior to the Civil Power.

HE has combined with others to fubject us to a Jurifdiction foreign to our Conftitution, and unacknowledged by our Laws; giving his Affent to their Acts of pretended Legiflation:

FOR quartering large Bodies of Armed Troops among us:

FOR protecting them, by a mock Trial, from Punifhment for any Murders which they fhould commit on the Inhabitants of thefe States:

FOR cutting off our Trade with all Parts of the World:

FOR impofing Taxes on us without our Confent:

FOR depriving us, in many Cafes, of the Benefits of Trial by Jury:

FOR tranfporting us beyond Seas to be tried for pretended Offences:

FOR abolifhing the free Syftem of Englifh Laws in a neighbouring Province, eftablifhing therein an arbitrary Government, and enlarging its Boundaries, fo as to render it at once an Example and fit Inftrument for introducing the fame abfolute Rule into thefe Colonies:

FOR taking away our Charters, abolifhing our moft valuable Laws, and altering fundamentally the Forms of our Governments:

FOR fufpending our own Legiflatures, and declaring themfelves invefted with Power to legiflate for us in all Cafes whatfoever.

HE has abdicated Government here, by declaring us out of his Protection and waging War againft us.

HE has plundered our Seas, ravaged our Coafts, burnt our Towns, and deftroyed the Lives of our People.

HE is, at this Time, tranfporting large Armies of foreign Mercenaries to compleat the Works of Death, Defolation, and Tyranny, already begun with cirumftances of Cruelty and Perfidy, fcarcely paralleled in the moft barbarous Ages, and totally unworthy the Head of a civilized Nation.

HE has conftrained our fellow Citizens taken Captive on the high Seas to bear Arms againft their Country, to become the Executioners of their Friends and Brethren, or to fall themfelves by their Hands.

HE has excited domeftic Infurrections amongft us, and has endeavoured to bring on the Inhabitants of our Frontiers, the mercilefs Indian Savages, whofe known Rule of Warfare, is an undiftinguifhed Deftruction, of all Ages, Sexes and Conditions.

IN every ftage of thefe Oppreffions we have Petitioned for Redrefs in the moft humble Terms: Our repeated Petitions have been anfwered only by repeated Injury. A Prince, whofe Character is thus marked by every act which may define a Tyrant, is unfit to be the Ruler of a free People.

NOR have we been wanting in Attentions to our Britifh Brethren. We have warned them from Time to Time of Attempts by their Legiflature to extend an unwarrantable Jurifdiction over us. We have reminded them of the Circumftances of our Emigration and Settlement here. We have appealed to their native Juftice and Magnanimity, and we have conjured them by the Ties of our common Kindred to difavow thefe Ufurpations, which, would inevitably interrupt our Connections and Correfpondence. They too have been deaf to the Voice of Juftice and of Confanguinity. We muft, therefore, acquiefce in the Neceffity, which denounces our Separation, and hold them, as we hold the reft of Mankind, Enemies in War, in Peace, Friends.

WE, therefore, the Reprefentatives of the UNITED STATES OF AMERICA, in GENERAL CONGRESS, Affembled, appealing to the Supreme Judge of the World for the Rectitude of our Intentions, do, in the Name, and by Authority of the good People of thefe Colonies, folemnly Publifh and Declare, That thefe United Colonies are, and of Right ought to be, FREE AND INDEPENDENT STATES; that they are abfolved from all Allegiance to the Britifh Crown, and that all political Connection between them and the State of Great-Britain, is and ought to be totally diffolved; and that as FREE AND INDEPENDENT STATES, they have full Power to levy War, conclude Peace, contract Alliances, eftablifh Commerce, and to do all other Acts and Things which INDEPENDENT STATES may of right do. And for the fupport of this Declaration, with a firm Reliance on the Protection of divine Providence, we mutually pledge to each other our Lives, our Fortunes, and our facred Honor.

Signed by ORDER and in BEHALF of the CONGRESS,

JOHN HANCOCK, PRESIDENT.

ATTEST.
CHARLES THOMSON, SECRETARY.

PHILADELPHIA: PRINTED BY JOHN DUNLAP.

INTRODUCTION

Peter S. Onuf

*T*HE DECLARATION OF INDEPENDENCE IS THE TOUCHSTONE of American nationhood, the document that marks the beginning of our history as a people. Eloquently articulating the principles and sentiments that drove patriotic subjects of King George III to resistance and revolution, the Declaration has served as a sacred text for subsequent generations of Americans. Other great state papers provided the blueprint for the national edifice, but none better defined the new nation's purpose. Americans have had—and certainly will have—a contentious and conflicted history, marked by ideological, sectional, economic, and religious strife. The federal Constitution itself inspired disagreement deep enough to unleash the "dogs of war" and threaten the survival of the union that the founders sought to perfect. Yet regardless of their disputes with each other, self-professed patriots have always proclaimed fealty to a common set of beliefs, invoking the principles so memorably epitomized in the Declaration: "that all men are created equal, that they are endowed by their Creator with certain unalienable Rights, that among these are Life, Liberty and the pursuit of Happiness.—That to secure these rights, Governments are instituted among Men, deriving their just powers from the consent of the governed, ..."

We now take these principles to be "self-evident." But what did they mean in 1776, when an objective observer might more accurately conclude that all men were created *un*-equal, and when the impartial historian would report that *no* government had *ever* been instituted on the basis of popular consent? And what about those "unalienable" rights that all men were supposed to enjoy but had been denied to virtually *every* people through history? Ironically, enlightened commentators agreed that the British were the only people to achieve a significant measure of freedom under law and security of their rights. For American loyalists who refused to abjure their allegiance to King George, the irony was more like tragedy. How, they asked, could American colonists secure their freedom by breaking with Britain, the historic source—and present guarantor—of their rights?

The refusal of a large number of colonists to embrace the Revolution—generally estimated at twenty percent or more of the total population—brings the Declaration's central

The Declaration was read in public squares and churches. A copy of the first Dunlap printing was sent to General George Washington, who had it read to his troops in New York on 9 July.

OPPOSITE: *Following the congressional vote in favor of independence on 4 July 1776, Congress ordered Philadelphia printer John Dunlap to prepare copies of the document for distribution the next morning. Because the New York Provincial Congress did not endorse a resolution for independence until 9 July, the Dunlap broadside simply announces "A Declaration," whereas later printings begin with the words "A Unanimous Declaration."*

riddle to the fore. Who exactly were the American people? How and when did they achieve a collective identity, a sense of themselves as a people that would enable them to declare independence, or for that matter anything at all? Again, the answer now might seem self-evident: as they made war against the king's armies, freedom-loving colonists were acting like "one people," assuming the sovereign prerogatives of the "powers of the earth." Thomas Paine and other impatient and impassioned patriots might well ask why it took so long for commonsensical Americans to come to terms with the facts on the ground. Their formerly beloved king had betrayed them.

Thomas Paine (1737–1809) was born in England but came to Philadelphia in 1774, where he lent support to the patriot cause as a writer and editor of political commentary. At the prompting of Benjamin Rush, he published Common Sense *in January 1776 to promote the idea of American independence. "There is something absurd," Paine wrote, "in supposing a continent to be perpetually governed by an island." Hugely popular, Paine estimated that some 150,000 copies of the anonymously signed pamphlet were printed. He directed his share of the profits to supporting the Continental Army.*

The long lapse of time between the opening of hostilities at Lexington and Concord in April 1775 and the Declaration in July 1776 is a measure of the profound ambivalence that gripped rebellious colonists who had taken up arms to vindicate their rights as Englishmen and who hoped to redeem their mother country and its empire from corruption and incipient despotism. The colonists originally resorted to violence because they were Britons, not because they were "Americans." Indeed, they only shared a common identity as Britons, for their immediate loyalties were to their particular colonies, provincial fragments of a greater Britain.

From our distant perspective, the Declaration seems to read clearly, with its "self-evident" "truths" still legible to us across the span of our national history. But if we look more closely, if we locate the act of declaring independence in its own time and place, everything begins to appear much different. National history constitutes the lens through which we look at the Declaration. As we focus on the origins of the new nation, "manifestly," irresistibly destined to world power—or so it appears in retrospect—some of the document's language passages seem pregnant with momentous meaning, while others fade into antiquarian obscurity, no longer relevant to us—or so we are now inclined to think.

This volume asks us to reread and rethink our founding document. The Declaration as we now understand it—the stirring passages that define our democratic creed—is not the Declaration that Thomas Jefferson and his congressional colleagues drafted, nor the document that inspired or provoked contemporaneous readers and listeners at home and abroad. Our goal is to make the historic Declaration come alive to modern readers, to enable them to hear what it had to say in its own time and what that unfamiliar document might have to say to us today.

We have assembled four of the Declaration's leading students to offer distinct, fresh, and complementary ways of reading its rich text.

Who wrote the Declaration and why were Americans across the continent ready

No one knows how many copies of the Declaration John Dunlap printed on the night of 4-5 July, but estimates range from 200-300 copies. Today, twenty-five are known to survive.

to receive its message? Pauline Maier suggests that focusing too obsessively on Jefferson's role obscures the crucial contributions of his congressional editors. Whether or not they improved the text—Jefferson certainly didn't think so—members of the Continental Congress collectively crafted a document that could speak for and to a heterogeneous and diverse patriot coalition. Most important, Maier shows, the congressional Declaration could not have gained widespread acceptance if colonists acting through local governments had not already been busily declaring themselves independent. That Congress spoke with one voice was crucial, but the "people" were already being heard as they forged bonds of union with one another.

What exactly did the Declaration say, and why was its message so compelling? Robert Parkinson shifts our attention away from the Declaration's familiar opening passages and asks us to consider the "twenty-seven reasons" for independence that were elaborated in the body of the document. Congress's decision for independence resonated with declarations across the colonies because patriots everywhere either shared grievances or imaginatively identified with victims of British despotism elsewhere. When George III made war on his soon-to-be former subjects, the charges became increasingly sensational. Atrocity stories that circulated in American newspapers provided grist for congressional propaganda, particularly those that linked the king with an unholy counter-revolutionary coalition of German mercenaries, "merciless savages," and rebellious slaves. The image of a people defined by war—and by its racial enemies—was codified by Congress in its catalog of grievances.

Why did Thomas Jefferson become so closely identified with the Declaration, and why is he now universally known as its "author"? The question, Robert McDonald maintains, concerns not simply who wrote what and the apportioning of credit. For the document to be effective, it had to ventriloquize the "people"—or at least the shared commitments of the signers, the people's delegates in Congress assembled. In fact, Jefferson's role as the Declaration's "penman" was scarcely known until the 1790s, and only gained wide currency when Jeffersonian Republicans needed to establish their patriotic pedigree and counter the Federalists' cult of Washington: if the first president was the father of his country, Jefferson was the author of its founding text. Jefferson's apotheosis was in turn facilitated by an emerging notion of authorship, linking the "genius" of a particular writer to "his" text.

The authors of the Declaration—whoever they might have been—envisioned a critically important role for the new American nation in world history. Yet who beyond America's ill-defined borders was listening, and what did they hear? David Armitage argues that the major obstacle to a present-day understanding of the Declaration is our failure to see it in its contemporaneous diplomatic context. The Declaration was a project, a bid for recognition that might have failed if rebellious colonists had not gained crucial support from foreign powers. Paradoxically, independence could be secured only through *inter*dependence and foreign alliances, not through the glorious isolation of a free people in their own new world celebrated by exponents of American exceptionalism. National self-determination depends on gaining a recognized place in the world of nations. Self-proclaimed peoples around the world have invoked the American declaration as a model and inspiration in their own bids for independence.

As our authors reread the Declaration from their various complementary perspectives, the richness and complexity of the text become increasingly conspicuous. There are no final, definitive, authoritative interpretations because the Declaration must always be read through the ever-changing medium of the national history it initiated. We can make sense of the Declaration only if we grasp the larger contours of our nation's history. Likewise, a historically attuned understanding of the document's production and reception in its own time can help us gain a clearer idea of who "we, the people" once were, who we have come to be, and may still become.

For the authoritatively edited text of the Declaration of Independence, see *The Papers of Thomas Jefferson*, volume 1, 1760-1776, edited by Julian P. Boyd (Princeton, 1950). See also *The Declaration of Independence: The Evolution of the Text*, by Julian P. Boyd, edited by Gerard W. Gawalt (Charlottesville, VA, and Washington, DC, 1999), which contains large color facsimiles of Thomas Jefferson's "original rough draft" and other copies and related compositional fragments and documents with an essay by Boyd on the drafting of the Declaration.

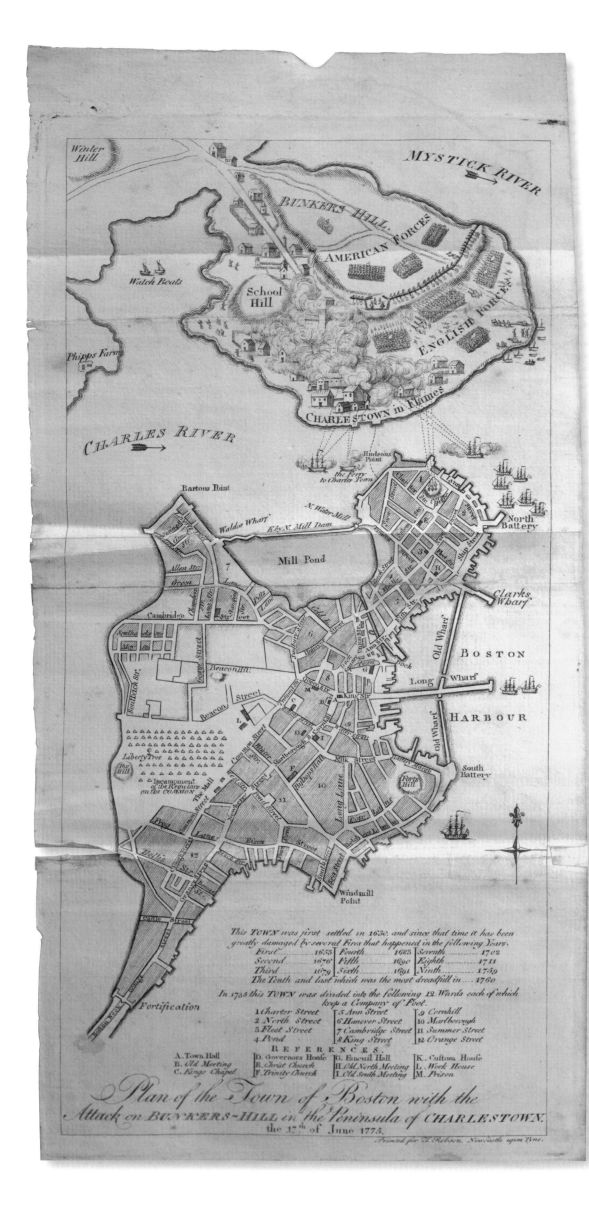

In June 1775, a British army of 6,500 occupying Boston was facing enclosure by a patriot force that had swelled to 18,000. To keep communication and supply lines open with his navy fleet and control Boston Harbor, British commander Thomas Gage moved his regiments to Dorchester Heights. American forces tried to prevent this move by occupying Bunker Hill on Charlestown Peninsula. Several assaults by the British forced the Americans, who ran out of ammunition, to quit the peninsula. Nevertheless, British casualties exceeded a thousand—twice the number suffered by the Americans—leading to debates in Parliament over the wisdom of King George III's design to suppress the colonial rebellion by force.

1763-1775

Prologue:

Britain's victory over the French in 1763 left it with a towering debt, and Parliament turned to the Americans to help ease the costs. The colonists vehemently protested the first effort—a stamp tax in 1765—and forced its repeal. Subsequent taxes escalated tensions; King George III responded by sending troops to Boston. This military presence spilled over into violence in the 1770 Boston Massacre. After the Boston Tea Party of December 1773, Parliament reacted swiftly with a series of Coercive Acts that closed Boston's port and put General Thomas Gage in charge. In April 1775, Gage moved to disarm the populace and arrest rebellious leaders Samuel Adams and John Hancock. On April 19, British troops marched to Lexington, where they clashed with the Massachusetts militia and touched off the Revolutionary War.

View of the Attack on Bunker's Hill with the burning of Charles Town, June 17, 1775.
A Boston Battery | B Charles Town | C British Troops attacking | D Provincial Rebels

1774–1775

King Declares Colonies in "Open and Avowed Rebellion"

The first Continental Congress met in Philadelphia in September 1774 to discuss how the colonies would respond to the Coercive Acts. They established a unified boycott and agreed to reconvene the following May. By the time the Second Continental Congress met, war had broken out in Massachusetts. The delegates soon established the Continental Army, with Virginian George Washington as its commander-in-chief. When news of Lexington, Concord, and Bunker Hill reached England, George III was determined to suppress the uprising. Rejecting Congress's "Olive Branch Petition," the king announced in August 1775 that his American subjects were "engaged in open and avowed rebellion."

1775 1776

January   February

January, 1776

Common Sense Published by Thomas Paine

Thomas Paine's _Common Sense_ appeared in January 1776. Employing everyday language, Paine made the case for independence in terms nearly all Americans could understand. The forty-six-page pamphlet became a sensation, selling more than 120,000 copies in three months. _Common Sense_ persuaded the colonists that monarchy was corrupt and that their cause was just and winnable. Paine was the first to lay blame directly at the king's feet, a radical indictment later made official in the Declaration of Independence.

June 7, 1776

Dissolving All Political Connection
In the Second Continental Congress, Richard Henry Lee of Virginia introduced a resolution for Congress to declare "that these United Colonies are, and of right ought to be, free and independent States, that they are absolved from all allegiance to the British Crown, and that all political connection between them and the State of Great Britain is, and ought to be, totally dissolved"—the first formal proposal for American independence.

June 11, 1776

Congress Nominates Drafting Committee
Congress nominated a committee consisting of John Adams (Massachusetts), Benjamin Franklin (Pennsylvania), Thomas Jefferson (Virginia), Roger Sherman (Connecticut), and Robert R. Livingston (New York) to prepare a declaration of independence. The group selected Jefferson to draft the document.

arch   April   May   June

Spring 1776

Relations between Britain and the Colonies Worsen
By the spring of 1776, relations between Britain and the colonies had worsened. The war was nearing its first anniversary, the king had rejected American attempts to seek a peaceful settlement, and rumors of a large, invading fleet of British troops and German mercenaries swept through the colonies. Bolstered by the ideas in *Common Sense*, more and more Americans saw independence as inevitable and called on Congress to sever all ties with Britain.

June 11–June 28, 1776

Drafting the Declaration
After nominating the Committee of Five, Congress recessed for three weeks. During this time, the thirty-three-year-old Jefferson—already an accomplished writer well regarded for his political pamphlet *A Summary View of the Rights of British America*—drafted the declaration with the help of Adams and Franklin. Much of Jefferson's language borrowed from other contemporary documents such as George Mason's Declaration of Rights and Virginia's new constitution. This engraving based on a historic painting by John Trumbull commemorates the presentation of the draft Declaration to Congress on June 28.

The Road to Independence: July 1776

July 2

Caesar Rodney's Dramatic Arrival Makes Vote Unanimous

Pressured by the arrival of a British fleet off the coast of New York, Congress called for a vote on independence on July 2. Caesar Rodney's arrival from Delaware that day made the decision unanimous among voting colonies; the New York delegation abstained. Turning to the task of approving an official Declaration of Independence, Congress then considered the language of Jefferson's rough draft.

July 5

Copies of Declaration Distributed on Horseback

On the morning of July 5, Dunlap's broadsides were dispatched to be posted and read aloud. The distribution of the broadsides prompted additional printings of the text in individual colonies from New Hampshire to Virginia. Through these printings, posted broadsides, and public proclamations, news of independence spread.

July 8

Dunlap Broadside Read in Public

Colonel John Nixon of the Philadelphia Committee of Safety read the text from Dunlap's broadside to the crowd gathered at the statehouse (later, Independence Hall)—the first public reading of the Declaration. With the broadsides being dispatched by messengers traveling by horseback, it would be many more weeks before the more distant colonies would hear the news.

2 3 4 5 6 7 8 9 10 11 12 13 14 15 16

July 1776

July 4

Declaration Officially Adopted

After two days of debate and revision, Congress officially adopted the Declaration of Independence. Working from the corrected manuscript, John Dunlap, Congress's official printer, produced broadsides of the text.

July 6

Declaration Text Appears in *Pennsylvania Evening Post*

The text of the Declaration first appeared in a newspaper when printer Benjamin Towne included it in his *Pennsylvania Evening Post*. It was preceded only by Dunlap's broadside printing.

■ July 9

New Yorkers Pull Down Statue of George III

Washington ordered the Declaration proclaimed to each brigade of the Continental Army, where it was received with "loud huzzas, and the utmost declarations of joy." That night, jubilant New Yorkers pulled down a statue of George III and had the lead melted into bullets.

■ August 2

Delegates Sign Official Copy

Delegates began to sign the official copy. Eventually fifty-six delegates signed their names, although not all were present on August 2. This engrossed Declaration is now on display at the National Archives.

18   19   20   21   22   23   24   25   26   27   28   29   30   31

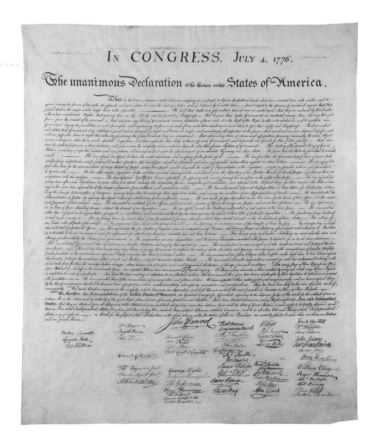

■ July 19

Congress Orders Official Copy

Congress ordered that an engrossed (officially inscribed) copy of the Declaration be produced on parchment. Timothy Matlack, assistant to Charles Thomson, secretary of Congress, likely performed the engrossing.

A FAC SIMILE OF THE ORIGNAL ROUGH DRAFT OF THE

Declaration of  Independence.

THE BODY OF THE WORK IN THE HAND-WRITING OF THOMAS JEFFERSON.—ALTERATIONS IN THE HADS OF JOHN ADAMS AND BENJAMIN FRANKLIN. ALSO, A FAC SIMILE OF THE SIGNATURES THERETO.

[The body of the document is a facsimile reproduction of Thomas Jefferson's handwritten rough draft of the Declaration of Independence, with handwritten alterations, followed by facsimile signatures including John Hancock, Rob Morris, Benjamin Rush, Benj. Franklin, John Morton, Wm Hooper, Joseph Hewes, John Penn, Wm Paca, Thos Stone, Geo Taylor, Samuel Chase, Rich'd Stockton, Jas Wilson, Geo Ross, Caesar Rodney, Geo Read, Th. Heyward Jun, Thos. Lynch Junr, Arthur Middleton, George Wythe, Richard Henry Lee, Button Gwinnett, Josiah Bartlett, Wm Whipple, Sam'l Adams, John Adams, Robt Treat Paine, Elbridge Gerry, Th Jefferson, Benj Harrison, Ths Nelson jr, Matthew Thornton, Step. Hopkins, William Ellery, Roger Sherman, Charles Carroll of Carrollton, Geo Clymer, Ja Smith, Sam'l Huntington, Oliver Wolcott, and others.]

WHO REALLY WROTE THE DECLARATION OF INDEPENDENCE?

Pauline Maier

*I*N 1826, THE YEAR OF HIS DEATH, THOMAS JEFFERSON composed his own epitaph, defining what he considered the greatest achievements of his life and the contributions to his country for which he wanted most to be remembered:

> Here was buried
>
> ### THOMAS JEFFERSON
>
> Author of the Declaration of American Independence
>
> of the Statute of Virginia for religious freedom
>
> & Father of the University of Virginia.[1]

Stipple engraving of Thomas Jefferson by Robert Field made in 1807 after an oil portrait by Gilbert Stuart (1755–1828) painted two years earlier. Field's engraving was sold as a separate print by the Boston publisher and various booksellers. Jefferson never received the original portrait, for which he paid Stuart one hunded dollars.

OPPOSITE: Brother Jonathan *was one of the nation's first pictorial weekly newspapers. This 4 July 1848 issue featured a full-page facsimile of Jefferson's "rough draft" of the Declaration. Images of the rough draft were increasingly reproduced during the mid-nineteenth century, when Jefferson's reputation as the document's primary author became more widely known and accepted. Brother John was originally a cartoon figure and symbol of America, like the later Uncle Sam.*

Jefferson had reason for claiming to be "Author of the Declaration of Independence." The committee appointed by the Second Continental Congress on 11 June 1776 to prepare a declaration on independence delegated to him the task of drafting it. Moreover, in the 1820s, when Jefferson asserted his claim to authorship of the Declaration, he still had in his possession what he called the "original rough draft"—actually a "fair copy," which is to say a complete version that he had compiled in June 1776 from compositional fragments on other bits of paper. On that "original rough draft," which is now at the Library of Congress, Jefferson recorded all subsequent changes in the text, including those by members of the drafting committee. Since most of those changes were in his handwriting, he might have assumed, understandably, that they were all made by him on his own initiative. He forgot that many of those changes were mandated by the drafting committee. He also failed to acknowledge the extent to which others had shaped the text that Congress finally approved on 4 July 1776 and made its authorship a title worth claiming fifty years later.

Jefferson did not seek the job that would become his primary claim to the esteem of posterity. After spending several months at Monticello, he finally returned to Congress on 14 May 1776. He then learned that Virginia was about to write a new state constitution. He wanted desperately to participate. The creation of new governments, he wrote, was "a work of the most interesting nature" and, indeed, "the whole object of the present controversy."[2] But Jefferson's colleagues on the Virginia delegation refused to let him go. After all, he had

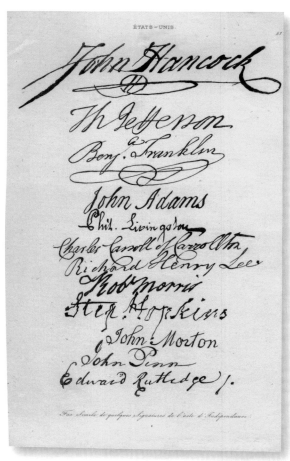

This facsimile engraving of selected signatures from the engrossed Declaration appears to be an illustration plate from a book published in Paris around 1800. As appreciation for the Declaration grew, its fifty-six signers and their autographs became objects of veneration.

just arrived in Philadelphia. It was their turn to go home. That didn't stop Jefferson. He composed his own draft constitution for Virginia, which he sent to the Virginia convention with two departing colleagues. It would arrive too late to make much difference: the convention used only Jefferson's preamble.

In the meantime, Jefferson received something of a consolation prize. During the congressional session on 7 June 1776, Richard Henry Lee, acting on orders from the Virginia convention, moved "that these United Colonies are, and of right ought to be, free and independent States, that they are absolved from all allegiance to the British Crown, and that all political connection between them and the State of Great Britain is, and ought to be, totally dissolved."[3] Congress discussed the resolution on 8 and 10 June, but decided to delay a vote until July because a substantial minority of delegations held instructions from their home colonies that prevented them from voting for independence. Opinion in those colonies was, however, "fast ripening," and soon they, too, would see the wisdom and inevitability of separation from Britain.[4] In anticipation of a positive vote, on 11 June Congress appointed what became known as the "committee of five" to draft a declaration on independence for its consideration. Its members were John Adams, Roger Sherman, Robert R. Livingston, Benjamin Franklin, and Thomas Jefferson, who served as chairman.

Adams later recalled that the committee had "several meetings, in which the members essentially outlined the document, proposing the Articles of which the Declaration was to consist, and minutes made of them" before appointing a draftsman to "cloath them in a proper Dress."[5] If Adams's recollection was correct, the committee essentially defined the shape of the document that Jefferson would draft.

In addition to the committee's outline, Jefferson had models to follow, which might explain why—if Adams again was correct—he was able to produce a draft in "a day or two."[6] It is clear, for instance, that Jefferson borrowed from the preamble to his own draft constitution for Virginia, which announced and justified Virginia's independence from Britain. That preamble, in turn, was modeled on England's 1689 Declaration of Rights, which had proclaimed the end of the reign of James II and offered the throne to his daughter, Mary, and her husband, William of Orange. The English document began with a "Whereas" clause. So did the preamble of Jefferson's draft constitution for Virginia, although it charged King George, rather than King James, with endeavoring to pervert the government of Virginia into "a detestable and insupportable tyranny." Both the English Declaration and Jefferson's Virginia preamble listed examples of the King's bad conduct, beginning each with the word "by." For example, Jefferson began Virginia's list of grievances with the words "by putting his negative on laws the most wholesome & necessary for the public good"—the same charge that, slightly rewritten, opens the list of grievances in the congressional Declaration of Independence. There, however, Jefferson began each grievance not with a "by," but with a more emphatic "He has …"[7]

Jefferson departed from his models in more significant ways in the opening paragraphs of the Declaration. In place of the legalistic "Whereas" clause, he began with the more lyrical phrase "When in the course of human events"—thus claiming for the Americans' struggle a place in world history so significant that "mankind" would have opinions on it. The second paragraph started with a very long sentence consisting of a series of distinct phrases beginning with "that" and culminating with an assertion of the right of revolution. Some of that sentence's most memorable words were adapted from an early version of the Virginia Declaration of Rights, drafted by George Mason and slightly modified by a legislative committee. That document appeared in the *Pennsylvania Gazette* on 12 June 1776, perhaps the day Con-

"The Drafting of the Declaration of Independence."

This idealized scene of the drafting of the Declaration, painted by American artist Jean Leon Gerome Ferris (1863–1930) in 1900, was popularly reproduced in many forms, such as this advertising card for Dr. D. Jayne's Family Medicines. The back of the card contains information about the firm and its products, as well as instructions for ordering an enlarged copy without advertisements for twenty-five cents.

gress's drafting committee first met. The Virginia draft stated "that all men are born equally free and independant [*sic*]." Did the committee ask Jefferson to incorporate Mason's language, or did he do it on his own? We cannot know for sure, but Jefferson clearly had to alter Mason's phrasing in order to fit it into the long first sentence of his second paragraph. On the "original rough draft," he wrote "all men are created equal & independent." He later crossed out "& independent."

In 1823, Jefferson recalled that once he had completed his draft declaration, he submitted it to John Adams and Benjamin Franklin "because they were the two members of whose judgments and amendments I wished most to have the benefit, before presenting it to the committee," and added that "their alterations were two or three only, and merely verbal."[8] He identified those changes in the margin of the "original rough draft."

Jefferson also claimed that after he submitted his draft with Adams's and Franklin's changes to the committee, the committee simply forwarded that draft, "unaltered, to Congress."[9] However, a letter he sent Franklin (who was recovering from gout, and probably did not attend any committee meetings) on a "Friday morn" in June 1776 indicates that the committee was far less passive than Jefferson remembered. "The inclosed paper has been read and with some small alterations approved of by the committee," he began. "Will Doctr. Franklin be so good as to peruse it and suggest such alterations as his more enlarged view

Portrait of Thomas Jefferson circa 1799 by Charles Peale Polk (1767–1822), a nephew of the more famous painter and naturalist Charles Willson Peale (1741–1827). The portrait was presented as a gift to the University of Virginia in 1965.

Below: *A replica of the writing desk on which Jefferson drafted the Declaration of Independence. Jefferson gave the original to his granddaughter as wedding present in 1825. It is now in the Smithsonian Institution.*

of the subject will dictate? The paper having been returned to me to change a particular sentiment or two, I propose laying it again before the committee tomorrow morning, if Doctr. Franklin can think of it before that time."[10] Not only had the committee defined the Declaration's structure, it also mandated "some small alterations" in its contents and so changed "a particular sentiment or two." The fact that the committee asked Jefferson to make those changes explains why they appear in his handwriting on the "original rough draft."

Meanwhile, between May and early July 1776, many towns, counties, and provincial legislatures wrote and adapted their own "declarations" on independence. Most of those documents were part of a widespread effort to allow or encourage Congress to proclaim independence. They include local resolutions endorsing independence and new state instructions to congressional delegations as well as declarations of independence for individual states. Except for the preamble to the Virginia constitution, there is no evidence that they influenced the wording of Jefferson's draft Declaration of Independence. These state and local declarations and resolutions, along with some critical maneuvers in a handful of state delegations, do, however, explain why the Continental Congress was able to adopt the Lee resolution on independence by a vote of 12–0 on 2 July. (The New York Assembly required its delegates to abstain from this vote, but officially adopted the resolution a week later.) They also allow us to evaluate Jefferson's success in providing "an expression of the American mind," which he later said was the Declaration's purpose, along with giving that expression "the proper tone and spirit called for by the occasion."[11]

Like Jefferson and their English ancestors, the anonymous draftsmen of these state and local declarations felt obliged to explain and justify their rejection of King George III. Sometimes they began, like the English Declaration of Rights, with a "Whereas" clause followed by a list of specific grievances. At other times, particularly in statements from towns and counties, they spoke more informally, even personally. At first they blamed Parliament and the ministry, as well as the king, for their grievances; later they put responsibility on the king alone, as Jefferson would do in drafting the congressional Declaration. It was the king, after all, who treated the colonists' petitions for redress with contempt and answered their prayers for "peace, liberty and safety under the British Government," as the freemen of Charles County, Maryland, put it, with "an increase of insult and injury." It was the king who had signed the Prohibitory Act of December 1775, which declared the colonists' "just resistance … to be rebellion, excluding them from the protection of the Crown, and even compelling some of them to bear arms against their countrymen" (Pennsylvania Assembly). "For the prayer of peace," the king had "tendered the sword; for liberty, chains; and for safety, death." He was also inviting "every barbarous nation whom he could hope to influence, to help him" in realizing his "inhuman purposes" (Boston). The colonists could not remain under a king who could "unfeelingly hear of the slaughter of his subjects, and composedly sleep with their blood upon his soul!" (Malden, Massachusetts).[12]

These attacks on the king, like those in Jefferson's draft declaration, formally announced that "the obligations of allegiance (being reciprocal between a King and his subjects) are now dissolved … by the despotism of the … king" (Pennsylvania Conference). Moreover, they expressed a conviction that the king was personally responsible for the Americans' grievances. One locality after another testified, like the citizens of Buckingham County, Virginia, that when the "dissensions first arose," their hearts were "warmly attached to the King of *Great Britain* and the Royal family," but "now the case is much altered." With

Six months before the approval of the Declaration, the Provincial Congress of New Hampshire ratified the first state constitution. New Hampshire was also the first state to hold a constitutional convention in 1778. On 5 June 1779, a state convention adopted a bill of rights and plan for a new state government, as outlined in this broadside printed by newspaper publisher Zechariah Fowle.

In the 1850s, Nathaniel Currier and James Merritt Ives formed a partnership to produce inexpensive hand-colored lithographic prints for consumption by the masses in an age when newspapers and magazines still could not reproduce photographs. Describing themselves as "publishers of cheap and popular pictures," Currier and Ives used production line methods to produce more than a million prints on subjects and events of all kinds. This 1875 Currier and Ives print depicts the five members of the Declaration drafting committee at work in a fictionalized setting.

"sorrow of heart" the freemen of Talbot County, Maryland, saw that "the King of Great Britain"—"the Prince we once adored" (Wrentham, Massachusetts)—was "inexorably determined upon the ruin of our liberties."[13]

To be sure, independence promised some advantages. It would bring new economic freedom, and freedom to found a new government with no king at all—a government where authority rested with the people most capable of governing America, the Americans themselves. But the colonists did not seek independence for those reasons. As they saw it, independence was forced upon them by the misdeeds of George III. Because of his actions, independence was not a choice but a "dire necessity" (Maryland); there was "no alternative left but an abject submission to the will of those overbearing tyrants, or a total separation from the Crown and Government of *Great Britain.*" The colonists had sincerely tried to preserve their connection with Britain, but were "driven from that inclination" by Britain's "wicked councils, and the eternal law of self-preservation" (Virginia). To support the truth of such assertions, colonists, like those of Maryland, appealed "to that Almighty Being who is emphatically styled the Searcher of hearts, and from whose omniscience nothing is concealed."[14]

Jefferson's draft declaration included no such invocation of divine authority. Indeed, it made only two references to God: the first paragraph spoke of "the Laws of Nature and of Nature's God," the next of a "Creator" who endowed men with "inherent and inalienable rights." During the two days they devoted to editing the draft on 2–4 July, members of Congress added the appeal to "the supreme judge of the world for the rectitude of our intentions" and statement of "a firm reliance on the protection of divine providence," and so made the Declaration a more faithful representation of the "American mind."

During those two days, as the British were assembling in New York the largest naval and military force ever gathered in North America, Congress eliminated fully a quarter of the text, drastically cutting Jefferson's overlong attack on the British people and eliminating his over-written and untenable charge that the king was personally responsible for the slave trade. It also removed several other questionable statements. The Americans did not want to "expunge their former systems of government," as the draft claimed, but only to "alter" them. After all, some aspects of British government, such as elected assemblies and trial by jury, were worth keeping. Nor was "the history of the present king of Great Britain … a history of unremitting injuries and usurpations," as if the man never slept. "Repeated injuries and usurpations" was more accurate. Congress also substituted phrases from the Lee resolution for parts of Jefferson's last paragraph and added the references to divine power and providence. However, it saved Jefferson's eloquent final pledge of "our lives, our fortunes, and our sacred honor." The result was a leaner, more powerful document.[15]

Jefferson did not appreciate the editing. He later made several copies of the committee's draft to show correspondents how Congress had mutilated his prose. (That was a fortunate move for historians: we would not otherwise know the contents of the draft, since the copy submitted to Congress on 28 June has been lost.) And yet by 1826, Jefferson readily claimed authorship of the Declaration. Why?

That transformation turned on a development beyond Jefferson's control. Beginning in the 1790s, Americans rediscovered the Declaration of Independence and gave it a new function as a statement of rights that had gone unexpressed in the Constitution and its first ten amendments, the Bill of Rights. Attention shifted from the final paragraph, which declared independence, to the opening part of the long sentence that began its second paragraph. Cut

A View of the State House in Philadelphia.

The State House at Philadelphia, meeting place of the Second Continental Congress, now known as Independence Hall.

The Continental Congress

Many colonists were angered by parliamentary efforts to raise revenues in British North America after the French and Indian War. When their petitions failed, they resisted their enforcement. Patriot leaders coordinated actions through correspondence networks and a series of continent-wide congresses, beginning with the Stamp Act Congress, which met in New York in October 1765.

Patriots boycotted, or, in the case of the 1773 Boston Tea Party, destroyed British goods to protest new taxes levied upon them. In response, Parliament passed the Coercive or "Intolerable" Acts to punish and restrain the colonies, particularly Massachusetts. To organize opposition, the First Continental Congress convened at Philadelphia in September and October 1774. Twelve colonies and provinces sent delegations. Once assembled, they negotiated rules to govern their proceedings. Each delegation was given a single vote, regardless of territorial, population, or delegation size. Delegation votes were determined by simple majority, as were congressional decisions, although on critical issues like independence members strived for unanimity.

The First Continental Congress created the "Continental Association," a program of economic sanctions intended to pressure Parliament into reversing its policies. The Second Continental Congress convened in May 1775, a month after war broke out in the Massachusetts towns of Lexington and Concord. Georgia sent a delegation in July 1775. To replace its original procedural rules, Congress sent the Articles of Confederation to the states for ratification in November 1777, but they did not go into effect until 1 March 1781. The Articles were superseded by the U.S. Constitution, which became operative on 4 March 1789.

off from the sentence's concluding assertion of the people's right to alter or abolish bad governments, which was fundamental to the Declaration's original role as a revolutionary manifesto, the sentence's opening words served its new purpose very well. They asserted the responsibility of an established government to protect the rights of its citizens. "We hold these truths to be self-evident," the passage began, "that all men are created equal; that they are endowed by their Creator with certain inalienable rights; that among these are life, liberty, and the pursuit of happiness; that to secure these rights, governments are instituted among men."

The process of culturally "editing" the Declaration continued after Jefferson's death. Abolitionists, members of the Republican Party of the 1850s and their leader, Abraham Lincoln, and others influenced its transformation on into the twentieth century, when a version of the passage above was engraved on the Jefferson Memorial in Washington, D.C. But the process had been well enough established by the fiftieth anniversary of Independence and the Declaration firmly enough implanted in the hearts of the American people that Thomas Jefferson, an old man worried about his place in history, could find consolation in claiming he was its "author."

How much do the contributions of others undermine that claim? Good writing often echoes other texts. Authors also generally get credit for the work of their editors, for which they are often as ungrateful as Jefferson. But what Jefferson wrote in June 1776 was not an essay, a poem, a story, or even an expression of his private convictions in the face of intense opposition, like his Virginia Statute of Religious Freedom. According to Jefferson's own words, he set out to write a public document that captured the "American mind." In that task he had the help of the elected representatives of the American people both on the drafting committee, whose contributions he happened to forget, and in Congress, which he wanted to forget. And his work took on a new life at the hands of generations of other Americans who reread the document and essentially edited it into a statement of rights and of the ideals that defined them as a people.

In drafting the Declaration, Jefferson did not anticipate that redefinition of its function. To be sure, he provided most of the text that subsequent generations used, and gave it a tone that helped it serve their very different purposes. But authorship of such a text was not, and is not, Jefferson's alone. The honor also belongs to the American people.

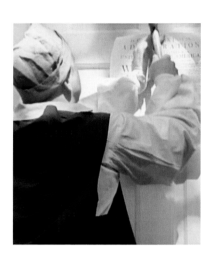

In the weeks following the congressional vote for independence, the text of the Declaration was printed in many cities and posted publicly. The broadside printed in Salem, Massachusetts (p. 61), included an order to read the Declaration at the conclusion of worship services in every parish of every denomination throughout the state.

--------------------- ---------------------

Suggestions for Further Reading:

The main themes of this essay are developed at greater length in Pauline Maier, *American Scripture: Making the Declaration of Independence* (New York, 1997). The essential documents for understanding the development of the Declaration's text are collected with extensive editorial commentary in Julian P. Boyd, ed., *The Papers of Thomas Jefferson*, I (Princeton,

1950). Boyd's *The Declaration of Independence: The Evolution of the Text*, revised edition, edited by Gerald W. Gawalt (Charlottesville, VA, and Washington, DC, 1999) includes splendid colored reproductions of several versions of the Declaration, including the "original rough draft." Jack N. Rakove, *Declaring Rights: A Brief History with Documents* (Boston and New York, 1998) is helpful in putting the Declaration's latter-day function as a statement of rights, not a revolutionary manifesto, in its historical context.

One of the winning competition drawings for the Jefferson Memorial in Washington, D.C., by architect John Russell Pope (1874–1937). Built in the neoclassical, rotunda-capped style that characterizes Jeffersonian architecture, the memorial was dedicated on the bicentennial of Jefferson's birth in 1943. Passages from the Declaration of Independence and the Virginia Statute for Religious Freedom are inscribed on the inner walls.

Notes

1 In *The Writings of Thomas Jefferson*, ed. Paul Leicester Ford, 12 vols. (New York and London, 1899), 10:396.
2 Thomas Jefferson to Thomas Nelson, Philadelphia, 16 May 1776, in *The Papers of Thomas Jefferson*, ed. Julian P. Boyd et al., 33 vols. to date (Princeton, 1950–), 1:292.
3 Ibid., 298.
4 Thomas Jefferson, "Notes of Proceedings in the Continental Congress," ibid., 309–11.
5 In *Diary and Autobiography of John Adams*, ed. L.H. Butterfield, 4 vols. (Cambridge, 1961), 3:336.
6 Ibid.
7 See the "Presentation Copy" of the British Declaration of Rights in Lois G. Schwoerer, *The Declaration of Rights, 1689* (Baltimore and London, 1981), 295–98, and, for Jefferson's draft constitution for Virginia, *Jefferson Papers*, ed. Boyd, 1:337–47 and also 415–20.
8 Thomas Jefferson to James Madison, 30 August 1823, in *Jefferson Writings*, ed. Ford, 10:267.
9 Ibid.
10 Thomas Jefferson to Benjamin Franklin, "Friday morn," *Jefferson Papers*, ed. Boyd, 1:404–6.
11 Thomas Jefferson to Henry Lee, 8 May 1825, in *Jefferson Writings*, ed. Ford, 10:343.
12 In *American Archives*, ed. Peter Force, 4th Series, 6 vols. (Washington, DC, 1833–46), 6:1018, 755, 557, 603.
13 Ibid. 6:963, 5:1207; 6:1020, 700.
14 Ibid. 6:1506, 461, 1524, 1507.
15 Edited Declaration in Pauline Maier, *American Scripture: Making the Declaration of Independence* (New York, 1997), 235–41.

Twenty-seven Reasons for Independence

Robert G. Parkinson

Americans have long interpreted, analyzed, and dissected the opening lines of the Declaration of Independence. Historians Carl Becker, Garry Wills, and others have contended that the preamble is the most important part of the Declaration and have wrestled with the meaning of its key words and phrases: "all," "men," "created," "equal," "pursuit of happiness," "inalienable rights," and "self-evident truths." Few, however, have given much attention to the twenty-seven reasons why the Second Continental Congress believed the establishment of an independent United States was justified—and necessary.[1]

Preoccupation with the preamble contrasts the reception of the Declaration by the "candid world" of 1776. British pamphleteer John Lind published *An Answer to the Declaration of the American Congress* that ran to one hundred and thirty pages. Of these, he devoted a hundred and ten to rebutting the list of complaints and grievances that the Declaration levied against Britain's King George III. A mere four pages toward the end addressed the opening paragraphs of the Declaration, only to dismiss them. "Of the preamble," Lind mocked, "I have taken little or no notice. The truth is, little or none does it deserve."[2] Sarcasm aside, he had a point: there was already a broad consensus among enlightened patriots concerning the ideas expressed in the preamble, including the consent of the governed and the right to revolution. Late in life, even Jefferson would admit that the Declaration did not aim at "originality of principle or sentiment."[3]

The list of the colonist's grievances, on the other hand, was crucial to the Declaration's immediate reception. It had to be both convincing and compelling. Long before future generations would revere it as a sacred text, in its time the Declaration was fundamentally a political document with pressing aims: it had to clarify a confusing military conflict, distinguish friends from enemies, inspire armed resistance, and garner sympathy (and aid) from European powers. Being now far removed from the turmoil, it is hard for us to understand the treacherous situation in which Congress approved and published the Declaration. While the delegates debated, edited, and ratified the Declaration, the largest invasion fleet ever assembled was already en route to New York. Their decision to use the

King George III (1738–1820) ascended to the British throne in 1760, in the midst of the French and Indian War. To help recoup the economic costs of the war, he imposed taxes and trade levies on the American colonies. Stubbornly dismissing their complaints, he determined to crush signs of rebellion.

Opposite: *On 9 July 1776, New York City's "Sons of Freedom" toppled the large statue of King George III on horseback that stood on Bowling Green. Pieces were transported to a foundry in Connecticut and melted down to make bullets for the Continental Army. During the European revolutions of 1848, Bavarian immigrant painter Johannes Oertel memorialized the event with a canvas that was engraved on copperplate (shown here) by New York printmaker and publisher John McRae in 1859.*

present tense to frame their accusation that George III "is, at this time, transporting large Armies of foreign mercenaries" surely reflected their worries about what might lie ahead. In fact, New York fell to the British commanders only a few days after independence was declared.

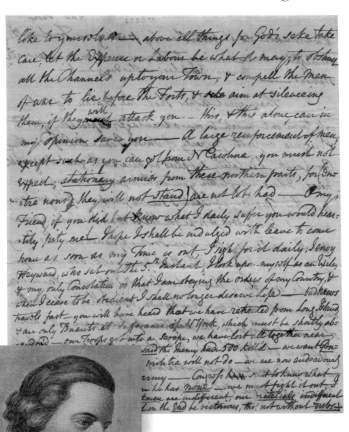

If the delegates expected thousands of Americans to put their lives at risk voluntarily, they knew they had to craft a manifesto that would lay out the reasons why. The twenty-seven charges leveled at George III were the heart of the matter. Originally Jefferson provided twenty-nine, but, during the editing sessions on 2–3 July, Congress cut two. The accusations were hardly assembled at random. Instead of presenting the evidences of the king's tyrannical oppressions chronologically, Jefferson grouped them thematically for maximum rhetorical effect. They begin slowly and then gain emotional speed. The first dozen detail the king's abuses of executive power, the next ten protest "pretended legislation," while the final five document acts of war and cruelty.

The twelve grievances that begin the list of facts and proof reach back a decade or more into the imperial crisis. They center on abuses of executive authority, accusing the king of multiple misdeeds, especially concerning the legitimacy of colonial assemblies and the authority of the laws they passed. Many refer to specific, local disagreements. The fourth charge, for example, reads: "He has called together legislative bodies at places unusual, uncomfortable, and distant from the depository of their public records, for the sole purpose of fatiguing them into compliance with his measures." John Adams, the powerful Massachusetts delegate who was one of the committee of five charged with drafting the Declaration, likely had Jefferson add this charge in order to voice Massachusetts's frustration with the forced removal of their assembly from Boston to Cambridge in the early 1770s. Yet, indicting the king for having caused fatigue and discomfort—or, as in the case of the seventh charge, for not encouraging British subjects to emigrate to America—could not have sufficed to inspire engagement in a bloody conflict. Furthermore, the relatively moderate tone of this section is sustained by the use of objective verbs: "obstructed," "refused," "affected." Nevertheless, toward the end of this initial group of accusations, Jefferson foreshadows his strategy of raising emotional tenor by invoking images of Old Testament plagues, accusing George III of sending "hither Swarms of Officers to harass our people, and eat out their substance."

The second group of grievances focuses on specific acts of the British Parliament and the king's willingness to enforce them. "He gave assent" to Parliament, the thirteenth charge declares, a "jurisdiction foreign to our Constitution, and unacknowledged by our laws," and

Revolutionary conflict highlighted the differences among Britain's colonies and dominions in North America. Canada and Florida were viewed as strategic threats to the patriot cause, and in 1776 much energy was directed—unsuccessfully—toward capturing the two territories. In this letter dated 14 September 1776, Declaration signer Arthur Middleton (1742–1787) of South Carolina discusses the Florida raid and expresses misgivings about war efforts in the north. "Bad news travels fast," he writes, "you will have heard we retreated from Long Island …"

Hamilton delin.

Noble sculp.

The Manner in which the American Colonies Declared themselves INDEPENDANT of the King of ENGLAND, throughout the different Provinces, on July 4, 1776.

Upon approving the Declaration, Congress ordered that it "be proclaimed in each of the United States." This image of the Declaration being read in public is based on an engraving first published in 1783. Like this example, it was reprinted frequently during the nineteenth century for celebrations of independence.

WHEREAS the STATE-CONVENTION in their Fifth Resolve recommended to the Inhabitants of the several Towns to keep a watchful Eye over each other, that no Evasion or Infringement of their Resolutions may escape Notice, and to enter into such other Regulations as they may think necessary to carry into Effect the Doings of said Convention: RESOLVED, That We the Inhabitants of this Town do hereby engage to watch carefully over each other, and ...sons with whom we have any Dealings, and whenever it shall appear to any of us, that an Offence against the Resolutions of ...ther ... said Conventions or this Town shall happen, we will report to one or more of the Select-Men or Committee of Correspondence, &c. ... impowered to make the aforegoing REGULATIONS, and carry the whole of these Resolves into Effect, who are to communicate to ...hole, and are hereby required to summon the Person accused before them, and him or them carefully examine, and if, after a fair and ...d Enquiry into the Case, it shall be determined that their Charge, or any Part of it is supported, and that he has knowingly and ...tionally violated these Regulations, then the Select-Men and Committee are directed to lay the whole Matter before the Town at ...cial Meeting called for that Purpose, in order that the Person or Persons so offending may be reprimanded---be published in ...News-Papers---be pronounced to have incurred the just Displeasure of the People---or the Influence of the Town used in ...ting the Government to transport him or them to the Enemy, according to the Nature and Degree of the Crime. ...HEREAS it may happen, from the Prejudices and Misunderstandings which subsist between some of the Members of every Com- ...ty, that Jealousies and Suspicions of each other will arise, which are founded on nothing but private Resentment :---To prevent, ...fore, the unmerited Sufferings of Individuals from such Cause, ...ESOLVED, That in all Cases of Complaint, where the accused on Examination shall appear to the Committee innocent of the Charge, ...riminal in so small a Degree as not to deserve public Censure, the Committee are hereby impowered to acquit such Person, who shall, ... such Acquital, stand fair with the Town as though no such Accusation had been made.   By order of the Select-Men, &c. *DANVERS*, AUGUST 26, 1779.   ARCHELAUS DALE, Chairman, Pro. Temp.

DANVERS: Printed by E. RUSSELL, at his Printing-Office, next the Bell-Tavern.   [Price 4/. by Hundred or Dozen. 4/ Single.]

As the Revolutionary War progressed, state and municipal governments took measures to police their populace and root out detracting loyalists. In this resolution published in the town of Danvers, Massachusetts, on 26 August 1779, citizens are advised to "keep a watchful eye" and report to one of the community's "select men" or its committee of correspondence any persons who appear to be subverting the patriot war effort.

supported its "pretended legislation." The following nine charges docket a menu of legislative acts that colonists deemed unfair, including each of the so-called Coercive or Intolerable Acts, the mercantile regulations that governed imperial trade, and the Quebec Act, which tolerated Catholicism and French law in the new British colony of Canada. Here we begin to see the principal American worries about encroaching British tyranny: suspending a colony's charter; keeping a standing army among the populace during peacetime; taxing without representation; and challenging trials by jury. To heighten the perception of these acts as an unceasing assault on American liberties, Jefferson abandons his device of blaming the king personally by beginning each accusation with a punctual "he has." Instead, charges fourteen through twenty-two advance in a steady cadence punctuated by colons. Rhetorically, they function as a single long sentence, embodying the sheer weight of oppression the American colonists had suffered during the previous decade.

Yet the real drama is still to come. Building toward a climax, the final five charges highlight the past year's violence. Jefferson's selection of verbs is now more evocative and stirring, and George's crimes more heinous: the king has "plundered," "ravaged," and "destroyed" his American subjects. He has forced them to become "executioners of their friends and brethren." He has recruited foreign mercenaries "to complete the works of death, desolation, and tyranny, already begun with circumstances of cruelty and perfidy, scarcely paralleled in the most barbarous Ages, and totally unworthy the Head of a Civilized Nation." These last accusations had to be decisive in their effect. Their acceptance by the "candid world," both at home and abroad, would determine whether American independence was legitimate and defensible—or not.

The delegates understood the rhetorical importance of the final set of charges. They labored over them more than all the other grievances during their editing sessions on 2–3 July. Other than rearranging a few words or slicing extraneous phrases, Congress allowed

Jefferson's first twenty grievances to enter the final Declaration mostly intact. As the stakes increased, however, so did Congress's attention. In several instances, the delegates amplified the king's crimes, adding emotional phrases such as "waging war against us" and the stinging if unsupported claim that his hiring of German troops went beyond all barbarity.

They also struck out two of Jefferson's accusations entirely as too controversial or confusing. The first charged George III with inciting loyalists to fight for the promise of gaining confiscated patriot property. The second was a long passage that blamed him for the crime of "waging cruel war against human nature itself" by promoting the slave trade and then doubly damning him for manipulating "those very people to rise in arms among us, and to purchase that liberty of which he has deprived them, by murdering the people upon whom he also obtruded them, thus paying off former crimes committed against the liberties of one people, with crimes which he urges them to commit against the lives of another." Yet blaming the king wholesale for the slave trade was deemed too tenuous—and dangerous—to include as the final, climactic accusation, so Congress eliminated that part of the charge.[4] The delegates retained the second part, however,

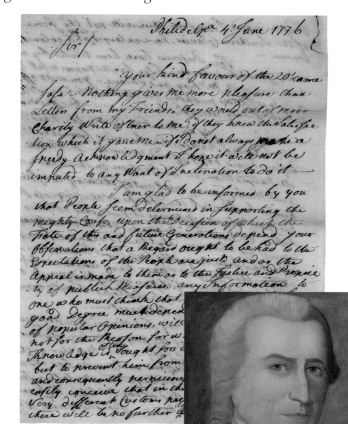

Each colony or state was responsible for contributing men and material to support the war. In this letter of 4 June 1776, Continental Congress delegate and Declaration signer Oliver Wolcott (1726–1797) expresses frustration about the amount of provisions his small "country" of Connecticut is expected to provide. A merchant and member of Connecticut's committee of safety, Wolcott was responsible for ensuring that the state's troops were properly supplied and administered.

with some important modifications. Whereas Jefferson had distinguished three categories among the groups that the Crown had enlisted to help put down the colonial rebellion—namely Indians, loyalists, and slaves—Congress removed the reference to the Tories and conjoined the actions of native and enslaved peoples to create a more succinct and powerful conclusion: "He has excited domestic insurrections amongst us and has endeavoured to bring on the inhabitants of our frontiers the merciless savages, whose known rule of warfare is an undistinguished destruction of all ages, sexes, and conditions."[5] This would become the twenty-seventh and final charge against George III, the ultimate justification for breaking from British rule.

This concluding charge was the product of widespread anxiety. In the sixteen months since the battles of Lexington and Concord, one of the most highly publicized concerns had been the role slaves and frontier Indians had played in the conflict. Newspapers throughout the continent kept their readers well informed about British efforts to enlist Indian support and attempts by royal governors to encourage slaves to abandon their masters and join the fight against them. Although most Indians had remained tranquil during the first year of the Revolutionary War, many colonists worried about what influence Canadian governor Guy Carleton and Indian agent Guy Johnson would have on the future of the conflict in the north. Meanwhile, the proclamation in November 1775 by Royal Governor of Virginia

Silversmith Paul Revere (1734–1818) made this famous copperplate engraving of the Boston Massacre of 5 March 1770 soon after the incident outside the customs house occurred. Patriot groups inflamed anti-British sentiment in the colonies with increasingly gruesome portrayals of the bloody scene.

Lord Dunmore, which promised freedom to those slaves who could reach his command, lent substance to the nightmares of many southerners. These two scenarios, which were widely feared in the months leading up to independence, were brought together in Congress's final grievance against the king.

The fearsome rhetoric of this ultimate accusation would have powerful consequences, casting a long shadow over the idea of who was "American," and who did not belong to the new nation. At the core of the Declaration lies a distinction between friends and enemies, Americans and Britons, patriots and King George III. The opening lines of the Declaration are the announcement of the separation of one people from another: "When in the course of human events it becomes necessary for one people to dissolve the political bonds which have connected them with another." Some who first heard the Declaration immediately understood the implication. After Colonel Arthur St. Clair read the Declaration to a cheering crowd at the already war-weary post at Fort Ticonderoga, New York, an observer commented that "it was pleasing to see the spirits of the soldiers so raised after all their calamities, the language of every man's countenance was, now we are a people!"[6] The ecstatic militia grasped the basic notion, but the underlying question was more complicated: who exactly were the American people?

The transfer of blame from Parliament to King George himself issued as a product of powerful rhetoric and argument. Tom Paine's sensational pamphlet *Common Sense* convinced thousands of Americans that they should revoke their loyalty to their formerly beloved King George. In the Declaration, Jefferson addressed the colonist's grievances directly to the king. He began most of the accusations with the phrase "he has," personally blaming the king for each injustice. George III, not his ministers nor Parliament, was America's enemy. Yet others fought on his behalf, most frighteningly rebellious slaves and Indian allies. When the Declaration connected these proxy fighters to the king, they also enlarged the definition of America's enemy to include those groups. Leaving no room for blacks or Indians who might otherwise have supported the patriot cause—and there were thousands who did—the Declaration portrayed them all as passive, mindless, bloodthirsty barbarians too naïve to realize they were being duped by a tyrant. *"We"* would never fall victim to such crimes. But who were *we*? The twenty-seventh charge implied that the *we* comprised those patriotic people who had the foresight and moral courage to resist the "repeated injuries and usurpations" of the "Present King of Great Britain." *We*—the American people—could not include the king nor his helpers, the "merciless savages" and "domestic insurrectionists."

At the crucial founding moment, therefore, the definition of an American identity was cast as a negative: not-British. But the heated language of the Declaration's twenty-seventh grievance gave it still another shape: not-black and not-Indian as well. At least one group of Americans understood this construction perfectly. At the same time that soldiers at Fort Ticonderoga brightened at the thought of now being a people, another crowd on Long Island's north shore gathered to celebrate the same announcement. They showed their approval for independence by constructing a visual representation of their multiple enemies. A newspaper report detailed the actions of the crowd that July afternoon: "An effigy of [George III] being hastily fabricated out of base materials, with its face black like *Dunmore's* Virginia regiment, its head adorned with a wooden crown, and its head stuck full of feathers, like *Carleton* and *Johnson's* savages, and its body wrapped in the Union [Jack] instead of a robe of state, and lined with *gunpowder*, which the original seems fond of." "The whole," the article concluded, "was hung on a gallows, exploded and burnt to ashes."[7] The crowd of Long Islanders simply acted out the text of the Declaration. By animating and then destroying the panoply of enemies arrayed against their new nation, they used fire instead of ink to attack and kill them. They consigned all their enemies—the king, the "merciless savages," and the "domestic insurrectionists"—to the flames, leaving the "Americans" to stand triumphantly and watch the blaze.

Exposing the king's tyranny, the twenty-seven grievances provided a negative identity against which the first semblance of a common national identity could be realized. That negative identity, however, intersected with long held prejudices against blacks and Indians that had grown up throughout the colonial period. To suit the particular political needs of independence, Jefferson and Congress played upon these fears "in the name, and by authority of the good people of the colonies." According to the logic of the Declaration, only after this ultimate, shocking breach of trust was pronounced could independence be justified fully, leaving Congress no choice but to declare the colonies free and independent states. By so doing, however, Congress fixed a devastating image at the very heart of America's founding document. The Declaration fastened racial prejudice to national identity.

We should therefore be wary of neglecting the list of grievances in our preoccupation and passion for the Declaration's more famous and familiar preamble. In its time, the core statement of grievances shouldered the burden of convincing beleaguered colonists and their allies across the Atlantic that the case for American independence was just and necessary. The final charge reflected an emerging conception of American identity, and of the new nation's enemies, that belied the soaring and optimistic phrases of Jefferson's opening paragraphs.

Opposite: *With this proclamation dated 12 June 1775, governor and commander in chief of the Massachusetts Bay province Thomas Gage established martial law while holding out amnesty to all rebels except Samuel Adams and John Hancock.*

Suggestions for Further Reading:

One exception to the general neglect by historians of the grievances section of the Declaration of Independence is Pauline Maier, *American Scripture: Making the Declaration of Independence* (New York, 1997), especially 105–23. For a rhetorical analysis of the Declaration, see Stephen Lucas, "Justifying America: The Declaration of Independence as a Rhetorical Document," in *American Rhetoric: Context and Criticism*, ed. Thomas W. Benson (Carbondale, IL, 1989), 67–130, especially 74–75, where Lucas contends that the Declaration comprises five principal divisions: the introduction, the preamble, the charges against King George III, the indictment of the British people, and the conclusion.

Notes

1   See Garry Wills, *Inventing America: Jefferson's Declaration of Independence* (Garden City, NY, 1978), Carl L. Becker (New York, 1956 [1922]), especially 202–3, and Jack P. Greene, *Imperatives, Behaviors, and Identities: Essays in Early American Cultural History* (Charlottesville, VA, 1992), 236–67.

2   John Lind, *An Answer to the Declaration of the American Congress* (London, 1776), 119. See also Wills, *Inventing America*, 65–66.

3   Thomas Jefferson to Henry Lee, 8 May 1825, in *Jefferson: Writings*, ed. Merrill Peterson (New York, 1984), 1501.

4   Congress did not, as Carl Becker reported, omit this passage "altogether" (see his *Declaration of Independence*, 213). For more on Jefferson's slave trade accusation see Pauline Maier, *American Scripture: Making the Declaration of Independence* (New York, 1997), 120–22; Wills, *Inventing America*, 72–74; and Paul Finkelman, "Jefferson and Slavery: 'Treason Against the Hopes of the World'," in *Jeffersonian Legacies*, ed. Peter S. Onuf (Charlottesville, VA, 1993), 190–92.

5   There is some scholarly debate over whom exactly Congress meant by "domestics." Stanley Kaplan believed that it was an explicit reference to Lord Dunmore's emancipation proclamation in Virginia, hence "domestics" meant strictly slaves; see his article "The 'Domestic Insurrections' of the Declaration of Independence" *Journal of Negro History* 61 (July 1976), 243–55. Stephen Lucas disagrees, contending that "domestics" was an umbrella term that included loyalists, servants, and slaves who were all disaffected to the patriot cause; see his article "Justifying America: The Declaration of Independence as a Rhetorical Document," in *American Rhetoric: Context and Criticism*, ed. Thomas W. Benson (Carbondale, IL, 1989), 109. For at least one contemporary critic, the answer to this question was obvious. John Lind wrote: "but how did his Majesty's Governors excite domestic insurrections? Did they set father against son, or son against father, or brother against brother? No—they offered *freedom* to the *slaves* of these assertors of liberty" (Lind, *Answer to the Declaration*, 107).

6   *New York Constitutional Gazette*, 12 August 1776.

7   *New York Journal*, 8 August 1776.

By His EXCELLENCY,

The Hon. *THOMAS GAGE*, Esq.

Governor, and Commander in Chief, in and over his Majesty's Province of MASSACHUSETTS-BAY, and Vice-Admiral of the same.

A PROCLAMATION.

WHEREAS the infatuated Multitudes, who have long suffered themselves to be conducted by certain well known Incendiaries and Traitors, in a fatal Progression of Crimes, against the constitutional Authority of the State, have at length proceeded to avowed Rebellion; and the good Effects which were expected to arise from the Patience and Lenity of the King's Government, have been often frustrated, and are now rendered hopeless, by the Influence of the same evil Counsels; it only remains for those who are entrusted with supreme Rule, as well for the Punishment of the guilty, as the Protection of the well-affected, to prove they do not bear the Sword in vain.

The Infringements which have been committed upon the most sacred Rights of the Crown and People of Great-Britain, are too many to enumerate on one Side, and are all too atrocious to be palliated on the other. All unprejudiced People who have been Witnesses of the late Transactions, in this and the neighboring Provinces, will find upon a transient Review, Marks of Premeditation and Conspiracy that would justify the fulness of Chastisement: And even those who are least acquainted with Facts, cannot fail to receive a just Impression of their Enormity, in Proportion as they discover the Arts and Assiduity by which they have been falsified or concealed. The Authors of the present unnatural Revolt never daring to trust their Cause or their Actions, to the Judgment of an impartial Public, or even to the dispassionate Reflection of their Followers, have uniformly placed their chief Confidence in the Suppression of Truth: And while indefatigable and shameless Pains have been taken to obstruct every Appeal to the real Interest of the People of America; the grossest Forgeries, Calumnies and Absurdities that ever insulted human Understanding, have been imposed upon their Credulity. The Press, that distinguished Appendage of public Liberty, and when fairly and impartially employed it's best Support, has been invariably prostituted to the most contrary Purposes: The animated Language of ancient and virtuous Times, calculated to vindicate and promote the just Rights, and Interest of Mankind, have been applied to countenance the most abandoned Violation of those sacred Blessings; and not only from the flagitious Prints, but from the popular Harrangues of the Times, Men have been taught to depend upon Activity in Treason, for the Security of their Persons, and Properties; 'till to compleat the horrid Profanation of Terms, and of Ideas, the Name of GOD, has been introduced in the Pulpits to excite and justify Devastation and Massacre.

The Minds of Men having been thus gradually prepared for the worst Extremities, a Number of armed Persons, to the amount of many Thousands assembled on the 19th of April last, and from behind Walls, and lurking Holes, attacked a Detachment of the King's Troops who not expecting so consummate an Act of Phrenzy, unprepared for Vengeance, and willing to decline it, made use of their Arms only in their own Defence. Since that Period the Rebels, deriving Confidence from Impunity, have added Insult to Outrage; have repeatedly fired upon the King's Ships and Subjects, with Cannon and small Arms, have possessed the Roads, and other Communications by which the Town of Boston was supplied with Provisions; and with a preposterous Parade of Military Arrangement, they affect to hold the Army besieged; while Part of their Body make daily and indiscriminate Invasions upon private Property, and with a Wantoness of Cruelty ever incident to lawless Tumult, carry Depredation and Distress wherever they turn their Steps. The Actions of the 19th of April are of such Notoriety, as must baffle all Attempts to contradict them, and the Flames of Buildings and other Property from the Islands, and adjacent Country, for some Weeks past, spread a mellancholly Confirmation of the subsequent Assertions.

In this Exigency of complicated Calamities, I avail myself of the last Effort within the Bounds of my Duty, to spare the Effusion of Blood; to offer, and I do hereby in his Majesty's Name, offer and promise, his most gracious Pardon to all Persons who shall forthwith lay down their Arms and return to the Duties of peaceable Subjects, excepting only from the Benefit of such Pardon, *Samuel Adams* and *John Hancock*, whose Offences are of too flagitious a Nature to admit of any other Consideration than that of condign Punishment.

And to the End that no Person within the Limits of this proffered Mercy, may plead Ignorance of the Consequences of refusing it, I by these Presents proclaim not only the Persons above-named and excepted, but also all their Adherents, Associates, and Abettors, meaning to comprehend in those Terms, all and every Person, and Persons of what Class, Denomination or Description soever, who have appeared in Arms against the King's Government, and shall not lay down the same as afore-mentioned; and likewise all such as shall so take Arms after the Date hereof, or who shall in any-wise protect or conceal such Offenders, or assist them with Money, Provision, Cattle, Arms, Ammunition, Carriages, or any other Necessary for Subsistence or Offence; or shall hold secret Correspondence with them by Letter, Message, Signal, or otherwise, to be Rebels and, Traitors, and as such to be treated.

AND WHEREAS, during the Continuance of the present unnatural Rebellion, Justice cannot be administred by the common Law of the Land, the Course whereof has, for a long Time past, been violently impeded, and wholly interrupted; from whence results a Necessity for using and exercising the Law Martial; I have therefore thought fit, by the Authority vested in me, by the Royal Charter to this Province, to publish, and I do hereby publish, proclaim and order the Use and Exercise of the Law Martial, within and throughout this Province, for so long Time as the present unhappy Occasion shall necessarily require; whereof all Persons are hereby required to take Notice, and govern themselves, as well to maintain Order and Regularity among the peaceable Inhabitants of the Province, as to resist, encounter and subdue the Rebels and Traitors above-described by such as shall be called upon for those Purposes.

To these inevitable, but I trust salutary Measures, it is a far more pleasing Part of my Duty, to add the Assurances of Protection and Support, to all who in so trying a Crisis, shall manifest their Allegiance to the King, and Affection to the Parent State. So that such Persons as may have been intimidated to quit their Habitations in the Course of this Alarm, may return to their respective Callings and Professions; and stand distinct and separate from the Parricides of the Constitution, till GOD in his Mercy shall restore to his Creatures, in this distracted Land, that System of Happiness from which they have been seduced, the Religion of Peace, and Liberty founded upon Law.

GIVEN at Boston, this Twelfth Day of June, in the Fifteenth Year of the Reign of His Majesty GEORGE the Third, by the Grace of GOD, of Great-Britain, France and Ireland, KING, Defender of the Faith, &c. Annoque Domini, 1775.

By His Excellency's Command,
THO'S FLUCKER, Secr'y.

THO'S GAGE.

GOD Save the KING.

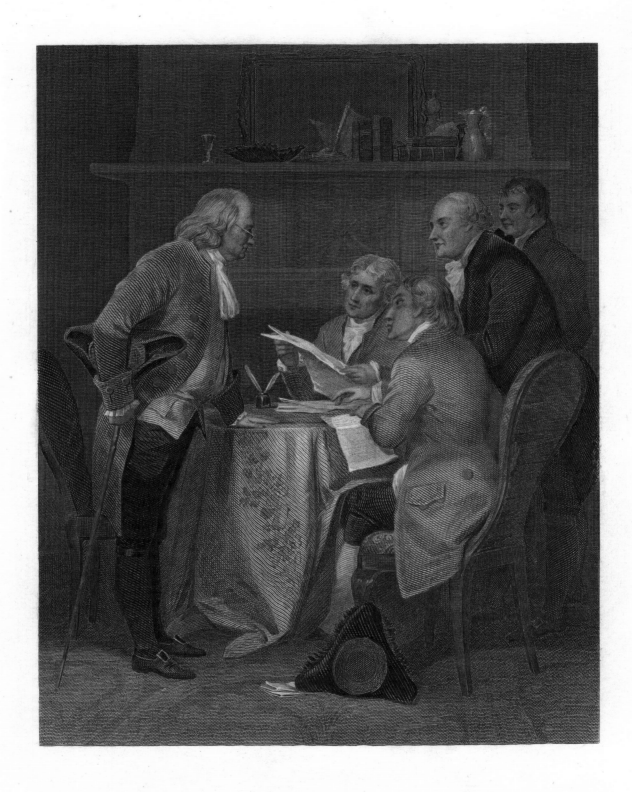

DRAFTING THE DECLARATION OF INDEPENDENCE.

THE COMMITTEE — FRANKLIN, JEFFERSON, ADAMS, LIVINGSTON & SHERMAN.

From the original Painting by Chappel in the possession of the Publishers.

Johnson, Fry & C.º Publishers, New York.

Entered according to act of Congress AD. 1861 by Johnson, Fry & Cº in the clerks office of the district court of the southern district of New York.

Thomas Jefferson's Strange Career as Author of Independence

Robert M.S. McDonald

*T*HE MOST BASIC "FACT" OF UNITED STATES HISTORY—that Thomas Jefferson authored the Declaration of Independence—was at first unknown to the public, became subsequently a matter of sometimes passionate dispute, and then only gradually a generally accepted premise.

Several factors explain Jefferson's initial anonymity as author of the Declaration. First, it was common for eighteenth-century political tracts to be published without a signature or to be signed with a pseudonym. The trio of James Madison, Alexander Hamilton, and John Jay, for example, authored their *Federalist* as "Publius." Benjamin Franklin wrote as "Poor Richard," "Silence Dogood," and "Richard Saunders." When Philadelphia lawyer John Dickinson argued against the 1767 Townshend Acts, he assumed the identity of "a Farmer."

One of the hallmarks of eighteenth-century republican thought was the belief that men who took part in the government of others should be "disinterested"—a term that Jefferson used to praise George Washington for resisting "motives of interest or consanguinity, of friendship or hatred." Disinterested men did not openly seek political influence, for doing so would make them suspect of seeking office for private gain.[1]

Authors who used pseudonyms or wrote anonymously not only wrote disinterestedly, they also showed their respect for the Enlightenment notion that an argument's authority came not from its author but rather from its logic. When Jefferson penned the Declaration, he invoked "self-evident" "truths." Similarly, Thomas Paine's *Common Sense*, which first appeared anonymously, contended that "who the Author of this Production is, is wholly unnecessary to the Public, as the Object for Attention is the *Doctrine itself*, not the *Man*." All that mattered, in other words, was the reasonableness of the argument, along with the reassurance that the author was "unconnected with any Party, and under no sort of Influence public or private, but the influence of reason and principle."[2]

Not just anyone could have succeeded so well as Jefferson in drafting a proclamation of independence for the Continental Congress. John Adams, who joined Jefferson along with Franklin, Roger Sherman, and Robert Livingston as a member of the committee

Jefferson's 1774 pamphlet A Summary View of the Rights of British America *elucidated the sentiments shared by many Americans about the British Parliament's perceived disregard of colonists' rights, and begged George III to mediate the conflicts between the dominions of his empire.*

OPPOSITE: *As public awareness grew of the role that Thomas Jefferson and other members of the Continental Congress played in shaping the Declaration, various artists set their imaginations to picturing scenes of the drafting committee at work. In this 1857 engraving made after a painting by Alonzo Chappel (1829–1877), Franklin, the elder statesman, is portrayed in the dominant role, with Jefferson, Livingston, Adams, and Sherman.*

charged to produce the Declaration, rebutted Jefferson's suggestion that he take the lead in writing the document by pointing out that "I am obnoxious, suspected, and unpopular. You are very much otherwise." Jefferson rarely participated in the contentious debates that made Adams "obnoxious." "During the whole Time I satt [*sic*] with him in Congress," Adams recalled, "I never heard him utter three Sentences together." What earned for Jefferson his colleagues' admiration was his "reputation of a masterly pen." Rhode Island representative Samuel Ward, for example, described Jefferson as "a very sensible spirited fine Fellow & by the Pamphlet which he wrote last Summer he certainly is one." The "Pamphlet" was Jefferson's 1774 *Summary View of the Rights of British America*, an anonymous tract that, after individuals in the Virginia legislature leaked their knowledge of his authorship, gained him notoriety as far away as London.[3]

Jefferson's status as a Virginian was also important. Because Adams's Massachusetts had borne the brunt of British abuses and been the primary scene of bloodshed during the early stages of the American Revolution, members of Congress could criticize anything that Adams might write in favor of independence as a product of not only personal prejudice but also local need. This, perhaps, is why Adams considered himself "suspected." On the other hand, because Jefferson's Virginia thus far had sacrificed far less to the rebellion, it

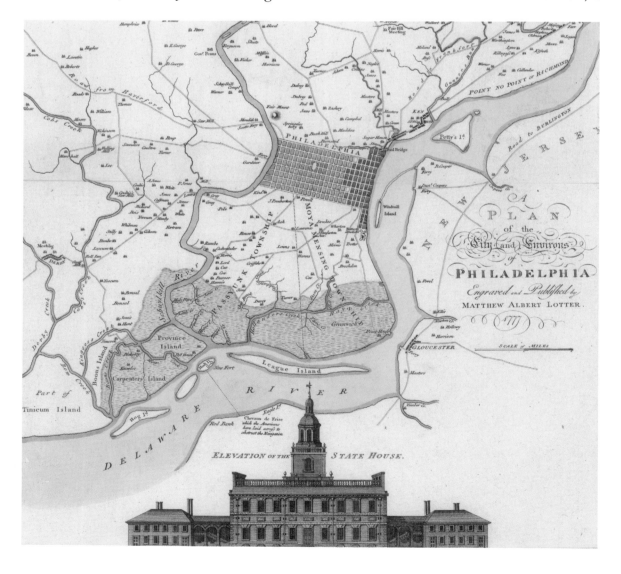

The Continental and Confederation congresses met in the Pennsylvania State House in Philadelphia, where the Declaration was debated, approved, and signed. Later called Independence Hall, this same building hosted the 1787 Constitutional Convention and the United States Congress from 1790–1800, when Philadelphia served as the nation's capital.

could presumably take a more disinterested stance. Furthermore, Jefferson, unlike Adams, had not yet publicly committed himself to the idea of independence. Even in the early summer of 1776, some members of the Continental Congress still argued against a formal break with the British government, and only a minority of Americans generally supported independence. As a result, the Declaration would need to rally not only Congress but a broader public to the cause. Adams, who told Jefferson that "a Virginian ought to be at the head of this business," understood that support from the most populous of the colonies—and the only southern one represented on the committee—was crucial to uniting Congress in favor of independence, and, through it, the rest of America.[4]

When Jefferson sat before his portable writing desk in his rented quarters on the corner of Philadelphia's Seventh and Market streets, he understood that the Declaration would be a group statement. The same was true of all resolutions of Congress, such as the 1775 "Declaration of the Causes and Necessity for Taking Up Arms," a product of the efforts of both Jefferson and John Dickinson, neither of whom received credit as author. But the Declaration of Independence, above all, would need to convey a sense of unity. "We" appears thirteen times in Jefferson's draft and ten times in the Declaration as altered by Congress. As adopted on 4 July, "A Declaration by the representatives of the United states of America, in Congress assembled" spoke "in the name and by the authority of the good people of these … free and independent states." After 15 July, when the New York delegation received instructions to vote for independence, Congress inserted the word "unanimous" in the title and deleted the reference to state "representatives," thereby strengthening the affirmation of consensus. Although the *Journals of Congress* listed the members of the committee appointed to prepare the Declaration, the records did not disclose Jefferson's particular contribution. More important than the proclamation itself was the courageous assertions it made, which the "unanimous" Declaration attributed to the "thirteen united States." Although Jefferson took pride in his text and felt pained when members of Congress struck out or rewrote portions of his draft, he understood and agreed with sentiments advanced that year by an anonymous pamphleteer: "No man is a true republican, or worthy of that name, that will not give up his single voice to that of the public."[5]

It is no surprise that Jefferson's fame as the scribe of independence would take so long to develop. At first, his contribution was known only to members of Congress. The earliest known public reference to his role as draftsman, a sermon published by Yale president Ezra Stiles in 1783, noted that it was Jefferson who "poured the soul of the continent into the monumental act of Independence." The recording in print of Jefferson's contribution hastened the dispersal of the information, which earlier had passed through conversations. Stiles, for example, recorded in his diary in 1777 that he had "Dined in Company with Col. [John] Langdon formerly of the Continental Congress. He says Mr. Jeffries of Virginia

Ezra Stiles (1727–1795), a Connecticut native and Congregationalist minister, served as president of Yale College from 1778 until his death. Stiles was the first to publicly identify Jefferson as the principal author of the Declaration.

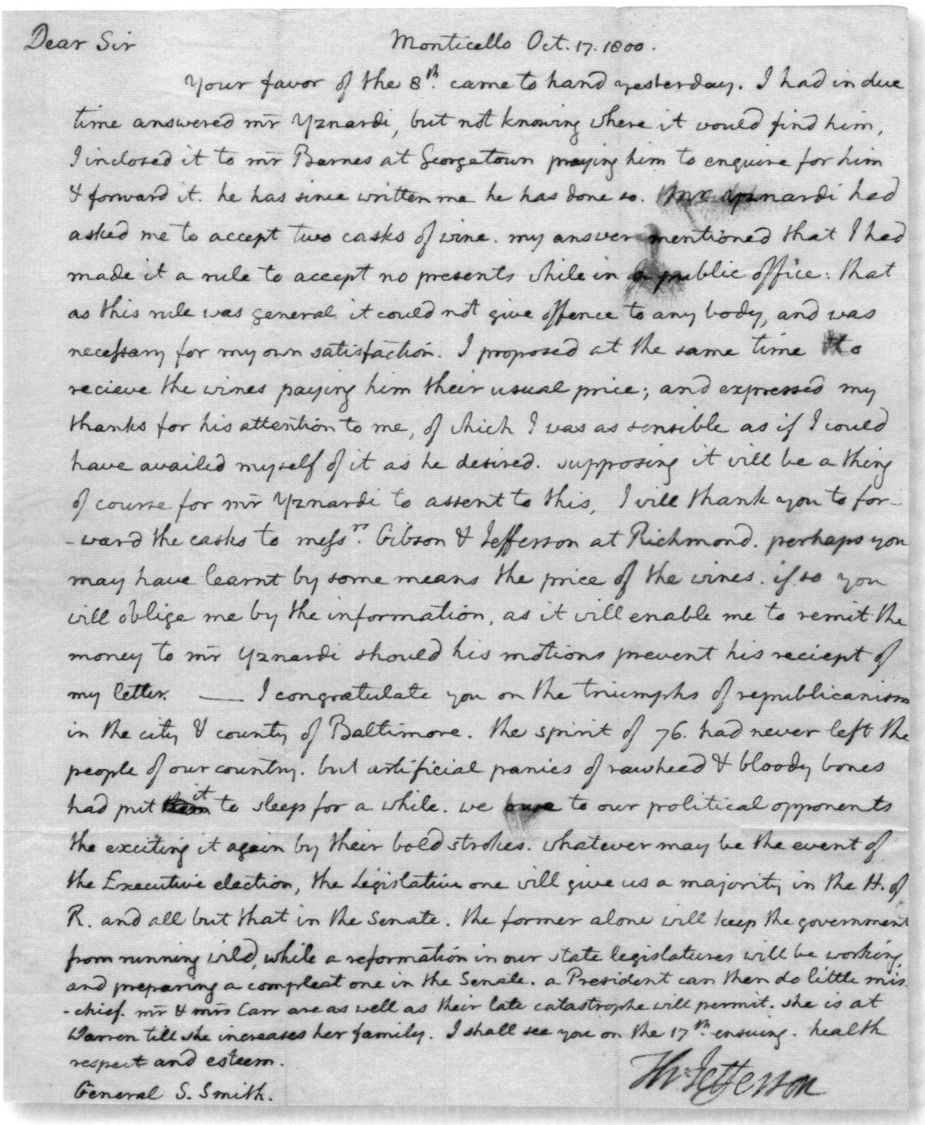

[Handwritten letter]

Dear Sir   Monticello Oct. 17. 1800.

Your favor of the 8th came to hand yesterday. I had in due time answered mr Yznardi, but not knowing where it would find him, I inclosed it to mr Barnes at Georgetown praying him to enquire for him & forward it. he has since written me he has done so. mr Yznardi had asked me to accept two casks of wine. my answer mentioned that I had made it a rule to accept no presents while in a public office. that as this rule was general it could not give offence to any body, and was necessary for my own satisfaction. I proposed at the same time to recieve the wines paying him their usual price; and expressed my thanks for his attention to me, of which I was as sensible as if I could have availed myself of it as he desired. supposing it will be a thing of course for mr Yznardi to assent to this, I will thank you to forward the casks to messrs. Gibson & Jefferson at Richmond. perhaps you may have learnt by some means the price of the wines. if so you will oblige me by the information, as it will enable me to remit the money to mr Yznardi should his motions prevent his reciept of my letter. — I congratulate you on the triumphs of republicanism in the city & county of Baltimore. the spirit of 76. had never left the people of our country. but artificial panics of rawhead & bloody bones had put them to sleep for a while. we owe to our political opponents the exciting it again by their bold strokes. whatever may be the event of the Executive election, the legislative one will give us a majority in the H. of R. and all but that in the Senate. the former alone will keep the government from running wild while a reformation in our state legislatures will be working and preparing a compleat one in the Senate. a President can then do little mischief. mr & mrs Carr are as well as their late catastrophe will permit. she is at Warren till she increases her family. I shall see you on the 17th ensuing. health respect and esteem.

General S. Smith.   Th: Jefferson

The presidential election of 1800 was a rematch of the 1796 election in which Federalist John Adams defeated Republican Thomas Jefferson by a narrow margin, making Jefferson vice president under the old system of electoral balloting. In October 1800, an electoral tie forced a run-off election in the House of Representatives, handing Jefferson the presidency and Aaron Burr the vice presidency. In this letter from 17 October 1800, with the outcome not yet known, Jefferson congratulated Congressman Samuel Smith (1752–1839) "on the triumph of republicanism" due to new legislative districting in Baltimore and surrounding counties, adding that "the spirit of '76 had never left the people of our country." Jefferson's election led to the demise of the Federalist party and a rift with Adams.

drafted the Declaration of Independency." Stiles's early confusion about Jefferson's name probably resulted from the fact that Langdon, too, was a secondhand source. Although Langdon left the Congress in 1775, he was a close friend of William Whipple, who had replaced him in the New Hampshire delegation and signed the Declaration the following year.[6]

Jefferson's draftsmanship remained obscure throughout the 1780s, in part because the Declaration itself had yet to take on canonical status. Americans who celebrated the Fourth of July as the anniversary of independence paid scant attention to the Declaration and even less to its writer. Dignitaries at a 1785 Independence Day dinner in New York, for example, toasted General Washington, soldiers who had died in combat, European allies, and "Liberty, peace and happiness to all mankind." No one raised a glass to Jefferson—and no one mentioned the Declaration. The earliest chroniclers of the nation's history, moreover, displayed similar indifference toward the Declaration and its authorship. Philip Mazzei noted only incidentally in his history of American politics that Jefferson, his longtime friend, had served as scribe of independence. William Gordon's 1789 history of the war and independence termed the Declaration an "act of separation from the crown of Great-Britain" and identified Jefferson only as one member of the committee that wrote it. Similarly, David Ramsay's *History of the American Revolution*, published the same year, ignored Jefferson and dryly described the Declaration as the "act of the united colonies for separating themselves from the government of Great-Britain." It was a means to an end of British rule, not a powerfully penned beginning of American government.[7]

Nevertheless, in the 1790s, after factionalism had polarized the newly constituted United States government and Jefferson had won recognition as a prominent political figure, partisans began to find new uses for the Declaration. At a time when Jefferson's enemies attacked his patriotism and questioned his commitment to America's ideals, supporters mounted a highly effective defense by linking him to the seminal expression of those ideals. A *National Gazette* writer, for example, sought public support for "Tom Jefferson" by noting that "he composed the Declaration of Independence" and claiming (not altogether accurately) that he "moved for it first in Congress."[8] At Fourth of July festivities, Republicans bolstered their ties to America's revolutionary legacy by heaping praise upon the Declaration, which—they frequently informed audiences—Jefferson had written.

The strategy worked. An embittered Federalist noted in 1802 that Republicans had successfully employed the Declaration "as a weapon in favor of the election of a man to the first office under our government." Indeed, while some credited Jefferson with merely drawing up the document, a growing number of people came to believe that he also had conceived it. At a Boston gathering on 4 July 1805, for example, Ebenezer French praised President Jefferson as "the immortal author of the DECLARATION OF AMERICAN INDEPENDENCE." In 1807, Levi Lincoln, Jr., of Massachusetts applauded Jefferson, "the sublimity of whose mind first ken'd American Independence and whose pen impressed the solemn Declaration." Three years later, Georgia's Steele White marveled at the skill with which the Virginian's "illumined mind could pen a 'Declaration of Independence'."[9]

Federalists, on the other hand, downplayed the connection between their nemesis and the nation's charter of freedom. Jefferson was merely the "reputed framer of the Declaration of Independence," John Lowell wrote in 1797. Less than a decade later, Supreme Court Chief Justice John Marshall discussed proceedings at the Continental Congress in his biography of Washington, burying in a footnote a tepid recognition that "the draft reported by the committee has been generally attributed to Mr. Jefferson."[10]

A few of Jefferson's enemies more forthrightly attempted to diminish the magnitude of his contribution. Grappling with issues of authority and authorship, they argued that credit for the Declaration—as well as the act of declaring independence—belonged to no single individual, but to all of Congress. "The assembled patriots of America declared" independence, Ezekiel Whitman reminded a Maine audience in 1801. Edward Bangs of Massachusetts concurred, telling a Worcester crowd that "our political fathers in Congress made that important and solemn declaration." The notion that the deed of writing the Declaration was not equivalent with the authorization of independence served Federalist purposes, but it also reflected the traditional understanding of the document as a corporate statement. Nonetheless, the novel and predominantly Republican conceptualization of the Declaration, which maintained that the ideas contained within the text originated with Jefferson, gradually gained ground and defined the terms of its subsequent reception.[11]

The apotheosis of the Declaration in the early decades of the nineteenth century made the issue of its authorship seem more crucial. Jefferson's detractors cast various doubts on any pretentions of authorial originality. Despite "repeated and positive assertions to the contrary," a Virginia Federalist testified in 1802, Jefferson "was not the draftsman of the declaration of American independence." An early version "had been drawn by *the committee*, not by Mr. Jefferson," he wrote, and then Congress made "essential alterations." By 1822, even John Adams had embraced the new conception of authorship. As Adams told

Timothy Pickering, "there is not an idea" in the Declaration that had not "been hackneyed in Congress for two years before." Richard Henry Lee had suggested earlier that Jefferson "copied from Locke's treatise on government." The so-called Mecklenburg Declaration of Independence, a possibly falsified document that emerged in 1819 and purported to signify the breaking of political ties with Britain by a county in North Carolina more than a year before the Declaration, further undercut claims of Jefferson's originality. Expressing similar principles and containing a number of phrases that appeared in his draft (such as "unalienable Rights" and "we mutually pledge to each other our Lives, our Fortunes, and our sacred Honour"), the Mecklenburg resolutions, as Adams wrote, either constituted "a plagiarism from Mr. Jefferson's Declaration of Independence, or Mr. Jefferson's Declaration of Independence is a plagiarism from these resolutions."[12]

Richard Henry Lee (1733–94), returned to Virginia soon after his 7 June 1776 resolution in Congress declaring the colonies "free and independent states" to help form his state's new government. He returned to Philadelphia in time for the 2 July vote on independence and later signed the Declaration.

Although Jefferson spurned the Mecklenburg tract as a hoax, he never claimed that his Declaration expressed novel thoughts or even that it expressed those thoughts with novel wording. "I did not consider it as any part of my charge to invent new ideas altogether," Jefferson maintained, "and to offer no sentiment which had ever been expressed before." The accusations that the principles contained within the Declaration had been previously voiced in Congress and set into print by writers such as Locke "may all be true," he admitted to James Madison in 1823. But "whether I had gathered my ideas from reading or reflection I do not know. I know only that I turned to neither book or pamphlet while writing it." Jefferson found himself in the odd and unenviable position of having new rules dictating authorial originality applied retroactively to a document written decades earlier, in accordance with older customs—customs that forbade him from taking credit even as composer, let alone author, but which also allowed him to borrow freely from others as he attempted to craft "an expression of the American mind."[13]

Jefferson dealt with this conundrum in various ways. He explained himself in private letters. He traced the evolution of the text of the Declaration in an autobiography written not, as he maintained, "for my own more ready reference & for the information of my family," but for posthumous publication. Finally, and in only one instance, he confronted his critics by claiming for himself the role of "Author of the Declaration of American Independence." He wrote those words for his tombstone.[14]

If in life Jefferson adhered to the public self-effacement demanded of members of his generation, he took care that his death would strengthen the link in the public mind between him and his Declaration. In the summer of 1826, as his health waned, he repeatedly expressed the hope that he would live to see the anniversary of the ratification of the document that he had penned fifty years earlier. Slipping in and out of consciousness, he awoke on the eve of Independence Day gasping, "This is the Fourth of July." "It soon will

The year before he died, Thomas Jefferson sketched a design for his tombstone and composed an epitaph in which he listed authorship of the Declaration first among the achievements for which he wanted to be remembered. The original grave marker was damaged by souvenir hunters in the mid-nineteenth century and donated to the University of Missouri for preservation. A replica (pictured) was erected in the family cemetery on Jefferson's Monticello plantation.

be," his physician, Robley Dunglison, replied. A few hours later, Dunglison roused him for a dose of medication. Believing that the Fourth had arrived, he whispered "No, Doctor, nothing more." At about noon on 4 July 1826—fifty years to the hour after the Declaration's approval by the Continental Congress—Jefferson died.[15]

Although Jefferson's role in drafting America's founding document went mostly unnoticed by his contemporaries in 1776, the final installment in the history of his life immortalized him for all time as its author. John Adams, on his own deathbed later that very same day, reportedly uttered as his last words, "Thomas Jefferson survives."[16]

Adams was wrong in one sense, but right in another. Jefferson and his Declaration of Independence did survive, and together they cast a long shadow over the American political landscape during the next half century. Americans would continue to reinterpret the role that Jefferson had played in producing the Declaration, and a few would continue to charge him with plagiarism. Yet their allegations tell us more about their own, more modern assumptions than they teach us about the lost world of the eighteenth century. So, too, do the abolitionists' claims that the Declaration's principles mandated freedom for slaves as well as the assertions of disunionists that Jefferson loomed large as the apostle of freedom for them but not for their slaves. Even though his forefathers had subscribed to the Declaration as a group assertion of secession and independence, Abraham Lincoln, in the 1850s, would embrace Jefferson for the rich lexicon of individual rights he wrote into the charter. Thomas Jefferson's strange career as author of the Declaration both reflected and reinforced the gradual and uneasy transformation of America itself.

Suggestions for Further Reading:

The main themes in this essay are developed at greater length in Robert M. S. McDonald, "Thomas Jefferson's Changing Reputation as Author of the Declaration of Independence: The First Fifty Years," *Journal of the Early Republic* 19 (Summer 1999): 169–95 and "Thomas Jefferson and Historical Self-Construction: The Earth Belongs to the Living?" *The Historian* 61 (Winter 1999): 289–310. On eighteenth-century print culture and rhetoric, see Jay Fliegelman, *Declaring Independence: Jefferson, Natural Language and the Culture of Performance* (Stanford, CA, 1993) and Michael Warner, *The Letters of the Republic: Publication and the Public Sphere* (Cambridge, MA, 1990). Jefferson's posthumous reputation is described in Merrill D. Peterson, *The Jefferson Image in the American Mind* (Charlottesville, VA, 1960, 1998) and Francis D. Cogliano, *Thomas Jefferson: Reputation and Legacy* (Charlottesville, VA, 2006).

Notes

1 John Dickinson, *Letters of a Pennsylvania Farmer*, as quoted in Gordon S. Wood, *The Radicalism of the American Revolution* (New York, 1992), 210; Jefferson to James Madison, 9 June 1793, in *The Papers of James Madison*, ed. William T. Hutchinson, et al., 17 vols. (Chicago and Charlottesville, VA, 1962–91), 15:27.

2 Thomas Paine, *Common Sense*, ed. Isaac Kramnick (New York, 1976), 64.

3 Adams to Timothy Pickering, 6 August 1822, in *The Works of John Adams*, ed. Charles Francis Adams, 10 vols. (Boston, 1850–56), 2:514; *Diary and Autobiography of John Adams*, ed. L.H. Butterfield, 4 vols. (Cambridge, Mass., 1961), 3:336; Samuel Ward to Henry Ward, 22 June 1775, in *Letters of Delegates to Congress, 1774-1789*, ed. Paul H. Smith, 19 vols. (Washington, DC, 1976–92), 1:535.

4 Adams to Timothy Pickering, op. cit.

5 Jefferson, "Notes of Proceedings of the Continental Congress" [7 June to 1 August 1776], in, *The Papers of Thomas Jefferson*, eds. Julian P. Boyd, et al., 33 vols. to date (Princeton, 1950–), 1:315–19; *Journals of the Continental Congress, 1774–1789*, ed. Worthington Chauncy Ford, 34 vols. (Washington, DC, 1904–37), 5:431, 590–91; *Four Letters on Interesting Subjects* (Philadelphia, 1776), 20.

6 Ezra Stiles, *The United States elevated to glory and honor. A Sermon preached before his excellency Jonathan Trumbull… And the Honorable General Assembly of the State of Connecticut… May 8ᵗʰ, 1783* (New Haven, 1783), 46; *The Literary Diary of Ezra Stiles*, ed. Franklin Bowditch Dexter, 3 vols. (New York, 1901), 2:155; *The Massachusetts Centinel and the Republican Journal* (Boston), 30 June 1784.

7 *Connecticut Courant* (Hartford), 11 July 1785; Filippo Mazzei, *Researches on the United States*, ed. and trans. Constance D. Sherman (1788; reprinted, Charlottesville, VA, 1976), 157; William Gordon, *The History of the Rise, Progress, and Establishment of the Independence of the United States of America*, 3 vols. (New York, 1789), 2:92, 105; David Ramsay, *The History of the American Revolution*, 2 vols. (Philadelphia, 1789), 1:340–41.

8 "Kibrothnataavah," *National Gazette* (Philadelphia), 12 September 1792.

9 "A Buckskin," *Virginia Gazette* (Richmond), 10 September 1802; Ebenezer French, *An Oration, Pronounced July 4, 1805, Before the Young Democratic Republicans, of the Town of Boston, in Commemoration of the Anniversary of American Independence* (Boston, 1805), 18; Levi Lincoln, Jr., *An Oration, Pronounced at Brookfield, Upon the Anniversary of American Independence, on the Fourth of July, 1807; Before a Numerous Assembly of the Republicans of the County of Worcester* (Worcester, 1807), 13; Steele White, *An Oration, Commemorative of American Independence, Delivered on this Fourth of July, 1810* (Savannah, 1810), 14.

10 [John Lowell], *The Antigallican; or, the Lover of His Own Country…* (Philadelphia, 1797), 49; John Marshall, *The Life of George Washington…*, 5 vols. (Philadelphia, 1805–7), 2:377n.

11 Ezekiel Whitman, *An Oration, Commemorative of the Day of the Declaration of Independence of the United States of America* (Portland, Maine, 1801), 11; Edward Bangs, *An Oration on the Anniversary of American Independence, Pronounced at Worcester, July 4, 1800* (Worcester, 1800), 3.

12 "A Buckskin," *Virginia Gazette*, 10 September 1802, reprinted in the *Richmond Recorder*, 29 September 1802; Adams to Timothy Pickering, 22 August 1822, in *Letters of Members of the Continental Congress*, ed. Edmund C. Barnett, 8 vols. (Gloucester, Mass., 1963), 1:516; Richard Henry Lee, as cited in Jefferson to Madison, 30 August 1823, in *The Republic of Letters: The Correspondence between Thomas Jefferson and James Madison, 1776–1826*, ed. James Morton Smith, 3 vols. (New York, 1995), 3:1826; Adams to William Bentley, 21 August 1819, in *Works of Adams*, ed. Adams, 10:383.

13 Jefferson to Adams, 9 July 1819, in *The Adams-Jefferson Letters: The Complete Correspondence Between Thomas Jefferson and John and Abigail Adams*, ed. Lester J. Cappon, 2 vols. (Chapel Hill, 1959), 2:543–44; Jefferson to Madison, 30 August 1823, in *The Republic of Letters*, ed. Smith, 3:1876; Jefferson to Henry Lee, 8 May 1825, in *Jefferson: Writings*, ed. Merrill D. Peterson (New York, 1984), 1501.

14 Jefferson, "Autobiography," [6 Jan.–29 July 1821], ibid., 3; Jefferson, Epitaph, [1826], ibid., 706.

15 See Nicholas P. Trist to Joseph Cabell, 4 July 1826, Cabell Papers, University of Virginia Library.

16 Charles Francis Adams, ed., *Memoirs of John Quincy Adams, Comprising Portions of His Diary from 1795 to 1848* (Philadelphia, 1875), 7:133.

OPPOSITE: *Like many ornamental engravings of the Declaration, this 1865 commemorative broadside of the Emancipation Proclamation features the full text of the decree surrounded by portraits of Lincoln and prominent abolitionists, images of the founding fathers, and vignettes of oppressed and liberated slaves.*

INDEPENDENCE DECLARED 1776.

THE UNION MUST BE PRESERVED.

WE DECLARE OURSELVES FREE AND INDEPENDENT

GENERAL WARREN

GENERAL LA FAYETTE

1. WASHINGTON. 2. JOHN ADAMS. 3. JEFFERSON. 4. MADISON. 5. MONROE. 6. J. Q. ADAMS. 7. JACKSON. 8. VAN BUREN.

The Columns are intended to represent New-England arising out of Old England, surmounted by Hope and Liberty;   The View is that of the Battle of Bunker Hill, from Chelsea, with Boston seen in the distance.   The main subject being General Washington surrounded by one Representative from each of the thirteen States—The National Flag of 1776, (a Pine Tree, on a white field), is on the right whilst the present one is seen on the left hand.

THE DECLARATION OF INDEPENDENCE IN WORLD HISTORY

David Armitage

No document in American history has shaped the world so decisively as the Declaration of Independence. Thomas Jefferson, writing shortly before his death in 1826, called it "an instrument, pregnant with our own and the fate of the world."[1] By that point, fifty years after the Continental Congress had first issued its Declaration, at least twenty other declarations of independence had appeared from the Caribbean, Latin America and Europe. Almost two centuries later, well over half the countries of the world have their own declarations of independence; many others still await recognition from the international community. All these declarations of independence can trace their ancestry back to the American Declaration of 1776.

When "the Representatives of the United States of America" announced that the United Colonies were "Free and Independent States," they did so in terms that were at once strikingly novel and reassuringly conventional. No public document had previously used the name "the United States of America": in this sense, the Declaration was America's birth certificate. Yet by calling the United States "free and independent," the Declaration's authors were using the standard criteria for statehood in the international law of the time. The United States may have been new actors on the world stage, but they would abide by the rules of international behavior and not pose a threat to the existing "Powers of the Earth."

The Declaration of Independence was meant primarily as a declaration of *interdependence*. The Continental Congress issued it to show a "decent Respect to the Opinions of Mankind." The bulk of the document consisted of a list of damning "Facts ... submitted to a candid World" to support the contention that the British king, George III, was a tyrant, and that resistance to him was therefore legitimate. If an unprejudiced world could be persuaded of the justice of the Americans' cause, then the colonies should no longer be subordinate to the authority of the British Crown, but rather stand as equals alongside the other powers of the earth—that is, the states of contemporary Europe, including France, Spain, the Dutch Republic, and Great Britain itself.

The immediate purpose of the Declaration in the summer of 1776 was not to declare a general right of rebellion against tyranny or to enumerate self-evident truths. As even

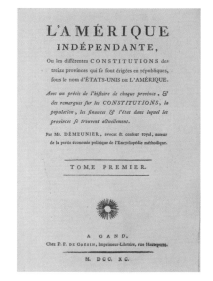

In 1790, French author and politician Jean-Nicholas Demeunier (1751–1814) published this collection comprising translations of America's state constitutions, the Articles of Confederation, and the Declaration of Independence to serve as inspirations and models for the newly formed National Constituent Assembly.

OPPOSITE: *This decorative engraving, featuring George Washington holding a parchment scroll representing the Declaration, was produced in the aftermath of the "nullification crisis" of 1832–33. Under President Andrew Jackson, Congress had implemented protective tariff laws that South Carolina deemed unfair and unconstitutional. Invoking states' rights, South Carolina adopted a formal ordinance delaring the laws null and void. A compromise was reached whereby Congress reduced tariffs while South Carolina rescinded its action, bowing to union supremacy.*

Abraham Lincoln later admitted, "The assertion that 'all men are created equal' was of no practical use in effecting our separation from Great Britain."[2] The aim instead was to turn colonies into states by transforming bodies of rebels within the British Empire into legitimate political entities with which other powers could engage diplomatically.

The Declaration's closing paragraph made its diplomatic aims abundantly clear: "that as Free and Independent States, they have full Power to levy War, conclude Peace, contract Alliances, establish Commerce, and to do all other Acts and Things which Free and Independent States may of right do." Thomas Paine, John Adams, Richard Henry Lee and others had been warning for months before July 1776 that no European powers would treat with the colonists so long as they were perceived to be traitors to the British Crown. "Honor, dignity, and the customs of states forbid them until we rank as an independant [*sic*] people," argued Lee.[3] Accordingly, on 7 June 1776, Lee moved a resolution in Congress "That these United Colonies are, and of right ought to be, free and independant states." Congress approved his motion on 2 July, and on 4 July voted to explain their action in the eyes of the world by means of a declaration of independence.

Within days of Congress's vote on independence, news of the decision began travel-

Not wanting to recognize American pretensions to independence, the British government did not issue any official response to the Declaration but instead secretly commissioned lawyer and pamphleteer John Lind (1737–1781) to publish a rebuttal. Printed in London, five hundred copies of the 130-page tract were shipped for distribution in the rebelling colonies. The accompanying "Short Review of the Declaration" was authored by Lind's friend, philosopher Jeremy Bentham (1748–1832).

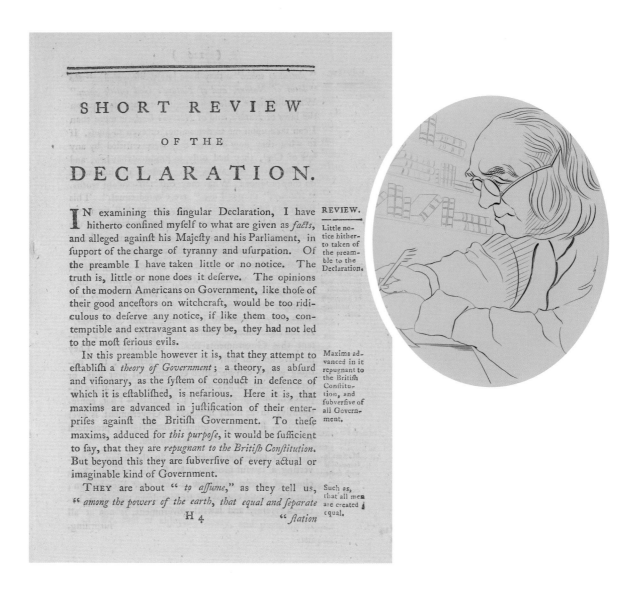

ing across the Atlantic Ocean. On 8 July, Congress sent a copy of the Declaration to its representative in Paris, Silas Deane, with instructions "to procure copies of it into French, … get it published in the gazettes," and circulate it to the French and other European courts.[4]

That first copy was lost in transit; a replacement did not reach Deane until November 1776, although two French translations had already appeared by then. In August 1776, news of American independence and copies of the Declaration reached ministers in London as well as newspapers throughout Britain and Ireland, the Dutch Republic and Austria. Within a few more weeks, Danish, Italian, Swiss, and Polish readers all learned what the Continental Congress had claimed, and many could read the Declaration, in whole or in part, in their own languages. Few documents in world history before 1776 can have traveled so far, so fast, as the Declaration of Independence.

The initial response from abroad, both political and diplomatic, was not as warm as the Declaration's authors might have hoped. Little commentary accompanied the various printings of the Declaration around Europe in 1776. The only two extensive published replies to the Declaration were hostile rebuttals that came from Britain, one by the exiled former governor of Massachusetts, Thomas Hutchinson (who thought the Declaration "a most infamous Paper"), the other by a young London lawyer, John Lind, and his friend, the budding philosopher Jeremy Bentham. Otherwise, silence mostly greeted the news of the Declaration.

Despite increasing opposition in Britain to King George III's determination to suppress the colonial rebellion by massive military force, the Declaration of Independence received little attention. Major newspapers, like the London Chronicle, *printed the entire text, but generally without explanation or comment.*

Congress was troubled by the lack of immediate interest from France. Understandably, the French court was waiting to see whether it would be prudent to support the Americans in their struggle against the British. Only in the wake of the American victory at the battle of Saratoga in October 1777 did France open the formal negotiations that would lead to a Treaty of Amity and Commerce with the United States in February 1778. With that agreement, the French became the first power effectively to recognize the Americans' capacity to contract alliances, establish commerce, and do everything that other free and independent states could rightfully do.

Though Britain would not formally renounce its claims to America until the treaties that ended the American War in September 1783, French recognition five years earlier had opened the way for others to treat the United States as an equal. In quick succession, the Dutch Republic, Spain, and powers such as Morocco entered into diplomatic relations. The Declaration of Independence had at last achieved its aim of introducing a new political actor among the powers of the earth: the United States of America, represented to the outside world by the Continental Congress. That, in turn, would be the beginning of the rise of the United States to become a symbol of liberation to others. As the French royal censor, the abbé Genty, put it somewhat extravagantly in 1787, "The independence of the Anglo-Americans is the event most likely to accelerate the revolution that will bring happiness on earth."[5]

The fortunes of the Declaration of Independence in the world beyond the United States rose and fell with the hopes of the oppressed, as well as with the fears of the authorities that ruled over them. As early as 1776, the British governor of Nova Scotia had censored the reprinting of the Declaration in the colony's newspapers; in the 1790s, authorities in Spanish America attempted to suppress the circulation of the Declaration and other American revolutionary documents. But the genie was already out of the bottle.

The first declaration of independence modeled on the American example appeared in 1777, on behalf of what would soon be called the state of Vermont. It was immediately resisted by New York—from which the secessionists were breaking away—and by the Continental Congress; Vermont would enter the union only in 1791. Such resistance foreshadowed what would become a striking rule of modern history: that those who have successfully declared their independence will then adamantly resist any further secession by peoples within their own territory, even at the immense cost of civil war (as in the United States between 1861 and 1865).

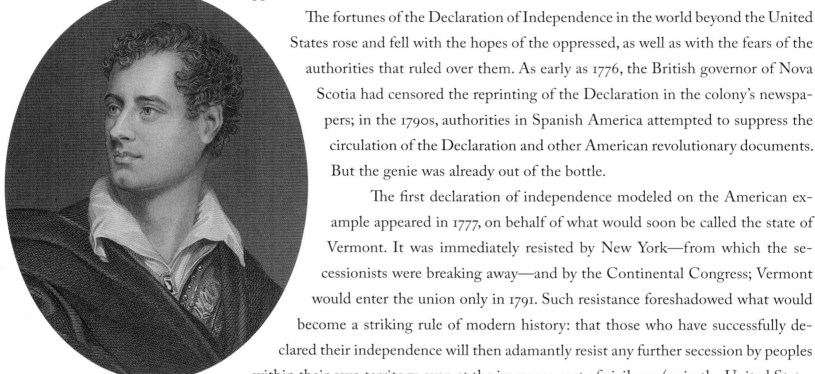

Incited by their love of classical Greek culture, poets and intellectuals like Lord Byron (1788–1824) embraced the Greek struggle for independence from the Ottoman Empire. In 1823, Byron went to Greece to fight alongside the revolutionaries. He died of fever a few months later. For his distinctive flair and dedication to their cause, Greeks revere him as a national hero.

In the wake of the French Revolution of 1789, the Declaration joined a group of novel documents proclaiming rights, both individual and collective, across Europe and the wider world. This language of rights animated movements for independence, autonomy, and liberation around the globe. As Lord Byron put it, in his celebration of the Greek independence movement:

> One common cause makes myriads of one breast,
> Slaves of the East, or helots of the West:
> On Andes' and on Athos' peaks unfurl'd,
> The self-same standard streams o'er either world.

Yet the Declaration itself would only gradually become a crucial component of that "common cause." In France after 1789, it aroused less interest among revolutionaries than the American state constitutions, which were translated and circulated in several editions. Its first imitation outside North America came from the Low Countries, where, in 1790, the Estates of Flanders concluded a summary of their historic grievances against the Austrian emperor Joseph II with language drawn from the Declaration: "this Province is and of right ought to be a Free and Independent State." Otherwise, its European impact in this period would be small compared to that of the French Declaration of the Rights of Man and the Citizen, for example.

1776. 1860.

DECLARATION OF INDEPENDENCE

Of the State of South Carolina,

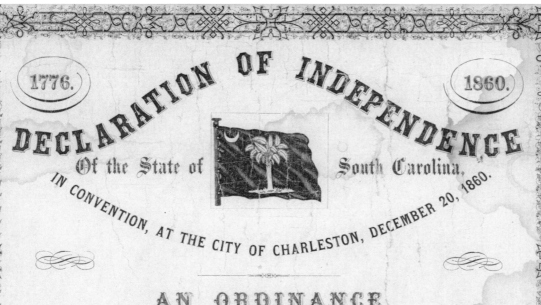

IN CONVENTION, AT THE CITY OF CHARLESTON, DECEMBER 20, 1860.

AN ORDINANCE

To dissolve the Union between the State of South Carolina and other States united with her under the compact entitled "The Constitution of the United States of America."

We, the People of the State of South Carolina, in Convention assembled, do declare and ordain, and it is hereby declared and ordained,

That the Ordinance adopted by us in Convention, on the Twenty-third day of May, in the year of our Lord one thousand seven hundred and eighty-eight, whereby the Constitution of the United States of America was ratified, and also, all Acts and parts of Acts of the General Assembly of this State, ratifying amendments of the said Constitution, are hereby repealed; and that the Union now subsisting between South Carolina and other States, under the name of "The United States of America," is hereby **Dissolved.**

D. F. JAMISON, Del. from Barnwell, President Convention.

THOS. CHILES PERRIN,
EDW. NOBLE,
J. H. WILSON,
THOS. THOMSON,
DAVID LEWIS WARDLAW,
JNO. ALFRED CALHOUN,
JOHN IZARD MIDDLETON,
BENJAMIN E. SESSIONS,
J. N. WHITNER,
JAMES L. ORR,
J. P. REED,
R. F. SIMPSON,
BENJ. FRANKLIN MAULDIN,
LEWIS MALONE AYER, Jr.,
W. PERONNEAU FINLEY,
J. J. BRABHAM,
BENJ. W. LAWTON,
JNO. McKEE,
THOMAS W. MOORE,
RICHARD WOODS,
A. Q. DUNOVANT,
JOHN A. INGLIS,
HENRY McIVER,
STEPHEN JACKSON,
W. PINCKNEY SHINGLER,
PETER P. BONNEAU,
JOHN P. RICHARDSON,
JOHN L. MANNING,
JOHN J. INGRAM,
EDGAR W. CHARLES,
JULIUS A. DARGAN,
ISAAC D. WILSON,
JOHN M. TIMMONS,
FRANCIS HUGH WARDLAW,
R. G. M. DUNOVANT,
JAMES PARSONS CARROLL,
WM. GREGG,
ANDREW J. HAMMOND,
JAMES TOMPKINS,
JAMES C. SMYLY,
JOHN HUGH MEANS,
WILLIAM STROTHER LYLES,

HENRY CAMPBELL DAVIS,
JNO. BUCHANAN,
JAMES C. FURMAN,
P. E. DUNCAN,
W. K. EASLY,
JAMES HARRISON,
W. H. CAMPBELL,
T. J. WITHERS,
JAMES CHESNUT, Jr.,
JOSEPH BREVARD KERSHAW,
THOS. W. BEATY,
WM. J. ELLIS,
R. L. CRAWFORD,
W. C. CAUTHEN,
D. P. ROBINSON,
H. C. YOUNG,
H. W. GARLINGTON,
JOHN D. WILLIAMS,
W. D. WATTS,
THOS. WIER,
H. I. CAUGHMAN,
JOHN C. GEIGER,
PAUL QUATTLEBAUM,
W. B. ROWELL,
CHESLEY D. EVANS,
WM. W. HARLLEE,
A. W. BETHEA,
E. W. GOODWIN,
WILLIAM D. JOHNSON,
ALEX. McLEOD,
JOHN P. KINARD,
ROBERT MOORMAN,
JOSEPH CALDWELL,
SIMEON FAIR,
THOMAS WORTH GLOVER,
LAWRENCE M. KEITT,
DONALD ROWE BARTON,
WM. HUNTER,
ANDREW F. LEWIS,
ROBERT A. THOMPSON,
WILLIAM S. GRISHAM,
JOHN MAXWELL,

JNO. E. FRAMPTON,
W. FERGUSON HUTSON,
W. F. De SAUSSURE,
WILLIAM HOPKINS,
JAMES H. ADAMS,
MAXCY GREGG,
JOHN H. KINSLER,
EPHRAIM M. CLARKE,
ALEX. H. BROWN,
E. St. P. BELLINGER,
MERRICK E. CARN,
E. R. HENDERSON,
PETER STOKES,
DANIEL FLUD,
DAVID C. APPLEBY,
R. W. BARNWELL,
JOS. DANIEL POPE,
C. P. BROWN,
JOHN M. SHINGLER,
DANIEL Du PRE,
A. MAZYCK,
WILLIAM CAIN,
P. G. SNOWDEN,
GEO. W. SEABROOK,
JOHN JENKINS,
R. J. DAVANT,
E. M. SEABROOK,
JOHN J. WANNAMAKER,
ELIAS B. SCOTT,
JOSEPH E. JENKINS,
LANGDON CHEVES,
GEORGE RHODES,
A. G. MAGRATH,
WM. PORCHER MILES,
JOHN TOWNSEND,
ROBERT N. GOURDIN,
H. W. CONNER,
THEODORE D. WAGNER,
R. BARNWELL RHETT,
C. G. MEMMINGER,
GABRIEL MANIGAULT,
JNO. JULIUS PRINGLE SMITH,

ISAAC W. HAYNE,
JNO. H. HONOUR,
RICHARD De TREVILLE,
THOMAS M. HANCKEL,
A. W. BURNETT,
THOS. Y. SIMONS,
L. W. SPRATT,
WILLIAMS MIDDLETON,
F. D. RICHARDSON,
B. H. RUTLEDGE,
EDWARD McCRADY,
FRANCIS J. PORCHER,
T. L. GOURDIN,
JOHN S. PALMER,
JOHN L. NOWELL,
JOHN S. O'HEAR,
JOHN G. LANDRUM,
B. B. FOSTER,
BENJAMIN F. KILGORE,
JAS. H. CARLISLE,
SIMPSON BOBO,
WM. CURTIS,
H. D. GREEN,
MATTHEW P. MAYES,
THOMAS REESE ENGLISH, Sr.,
ALBERTUS CHAMBERS SPAIN,
J. M. GADBERRY,
J. S. SIMS,
WM. H. GIST,
JAMES JEFFERIES,
ANTHONY W. DOZIER,
JOHN G. PRESSLEY,
R. C. LOGAN,
FRANCIS S. PARKER,
BENJ. FANEUIL DUNKIN,
SAMUEL TAYLOR ATKINSON,
ALEX. M. FORSTER,
WM. BLACKBURN WILSON,
ROBERT T. ALLISON,
SAMUEL RAINEY,
A. BAXTER SPRINGS,
A. I. BARRON,
A. T. DARBY.

EVANS & COGSWELL, PRINTERS, 3 BROAD STREET, CHARLESTON.

Seizing on the principle expressed in the Declaration "that whenever any form of government becomes destructive of the ends for which it was established, it is the right of the people to alter or abolish it, and to institute a new government," South Carolina declared its secession and independence from the United States on 20 December 1860—an action that soon led to the outbreak of hostilities with the federal union forces at Fort Sumter and the beginning of the Civil War. South Carolina regarded efforts by northern states to abolish slavery an abrogation of constitutional protections of states' rights respecting property.

THE UNITED — ESTATES

THE UNITED
OF LABOR, AGRICULTURE, COMMERCE,
And all other Professions
IN CONGRESS ASSEMBLED,
UNANIMOUS

ESTATES
THE MECHANIC AND LIBERAL ARTS.
And Occupations of Life,
PROMULGATE THE FOLLOWING
DECLARATION OF

TEMPERANCE.

When, in the course of moral events, the people of this enlightened age, are determined to burst asunder the intemperate bonds which have bound them down, and to assume upon the earth the moral, social and physical condition, to which the laws of Nature and of nature's God entitle them, an affectionate concern, for the well-being of their race, a sublime instinct of the love of country, and a profound sentiment of self-respect, require that they should fearlessly, declare the causes, which impel them to adopt Total Abstinence. We hold these truths to be self-evident, that all men are born sober; that they are endowed by their creator with certain faculties of the mind and body, existing in a mysterious union. That among these are life, health, liberty, and the pursuit of happiness. That to secure and perpetuate these rights temperance should prevail amongst men.

And as the habit of drinking intoxicating liquors becomes destructive to these ends; it is the right and duty of a people to abolish the use of them; for that should be abolished forever, that forever generates abuses. Our only drink should be pure water, which flows from the bosom of our mother earth, and is beneficently provided by a wise providence, to slake our thirst in the best way, for our health, happiness, and prosperity.

The iron rule of habit, when once established, is difficult of change. But with the stout heart of decision, we will shake off the terrible one of intemperance; for the time has come, when we will not suffer bad things because our fathers suffered worse. We will drive from the fair fields of our country, King Alcohol, and route his dissipated forces. The history of this dark despot, and his spirited ministers Rum, Whiskey, Gin, and Brandy, is a history of repeated injuries, all tending to our ruin. To prove this let facts be submitted to a candid world.

The Creator of this lovely globe, which we inhabit, encircled it with rays of genial climate, congenial to the growth of the innumerable classes of plants with which it is clothed. The mountain gives its sweet herbage, and the meadow its juicy grass, for the support of the ruminating animals which are reared for our solid food. The golden fields wave with corn, wheat, and rye, for our bread-stuffs; below ground vegetates the potatoe, and other edible roots, for our nutriment.

To these substantial viands of creation a gracious Providence has added a dessert. From the rich fruits and brimming nectar cup of Nature; in her rustic basket, we have the melting peach, the apple, pear, plum, quince and cherry, with their sunny rivals of the tropics. On her board, the towering palm flows with its cooling beverage,—the ripe olive melts with oil,—the golden cane drips with its ambrosial sweets, and the dewy vine hangs with its swelling clusters; together with aromatic conserves and lively cordials, alike grateful to the palate and cheering to the spirit; and the pure essences of unnumbered spicy trees and plants, glowing with flowers, leaves, and berries.

We say it is the first cruel wrong of king Alcohol, assisted by his prime minister, the Distiller, that they forage with a spirit more ruthless and terrible, than the invading armies of Bonaparte, and seize on the ruddy orchard, the flowering garden, the full-eared harvest, and turn the sober juice and very blood of Nature into a subtle poison, which has ruin in its taste and death in the draught.

We accuse this despot, and his accessaries, those who distill and traffic in ardent spirits, of marching through the land, both day and night, with sleepless activity; destroying industry, rearing poor-houses, and augmenting taxation; squandering property; undermining vigor; engendering disease; paralizing intellect; impairing moral principle, and "changing a fair, healthy, robust frame for a shrinking, suffering, living corpse, with nothing of vitality but the power of suffering, and with everything of death but its peace."

He has caused many an aged parent to weep over the downward course of a son, around whose staggering path the shadows of early death are fast closing. Over his earliest years they hung with hope and rapture, as they pressed "the velvet lip of infancy," and kissed the rosy cheek of childhood with its sparkling eye, and watched the vigorous budding of intellect and beauty. But, now, alas! how the scene is changed; when with agony they behold him with his blistered lip,—tainted breath,—inflamed eye,—swollen cheek,—trembling limbs, and benumbed faculties. And, finally, when the scene is closed, and the clod of the valley covers his bloated form, they feel a horrid satisfaction that his grave is no farther from his cradle.

He has caused the heart-broken wife to keep her midnight watchings over her sick and supperless children, "as, with a countenance haggard with care and woe, she seeks in vain to supply the wants of a half-starved, sickly, shrieking babe out of the fountain which hunger, and ill usage, and despair, have exhausted." Where is her husband? Where is the once "ardent lover, whose graces won her from the home of her infancy?—the enraptured father, who bent with such delight over his new-born children," and should now appease the gnawings of hunger and administer to the sufferings of his unhappy offspring? Unfortunate and wretched man! with all the finer feelings of his nature blasted by the fierce sirocco of intemperance, he is now carousing at the neighboring dram shop, or, overcome by Alcohol, is asleep in the road-side.

He has caused the lonely widow to faint at her toilsome labor, as her children cry for bread which she is unable to procure; whilst he, who might still have been living, to provide for and protect them, and be repaid by their love and fondest affection, has rolled into a drunkard's grave.

He has driven the timid infant from home, and wrenched his young heart's fibres by leaving him in his helplessness, alone among strangers.

He has clothed the orphan in rags, and scattered brothers and sisters to the four quarters of the land.

He has caused our houses to become dilapidated; the roofs to leak; the windows broken; the doors unhinged, and the winds to blow across the desolate hearths.

He has caused our farms to become impoverished; the barns empty; the cattle driven away; the crops neglected; the fences broken down; the fields covered with noxious weeds, and the pastures with thorny bushes.

He has retarded the progress of education, and banished knowledge, that fairest daughter of heaven.

He has festered the pure and mantling blood of patriotism, and soiled the star-striped cap of liberty with its eagle plumes.

He has withered the rosy and myrtled wreaths of love and friendship, which were in ethereal bloom, and fragrant from the dew, scattered on them by the wings of angels.

He has extinguished the light of our holy religion; that sacred principle which gives us fortitude and patience under calamities, disappointments and suffering resolution to withstand temptations,—meekness and humility in the enjoyment of honor and fortune; that religion whose exalting and consoling influences are adapted to the noblest faculties of our nature. It gives the only true happiness in this life, and, in the hour of death, when all human aid and hope fails, it throws around the Christian the bright and serene rays of faith and resignation, to illumine the way of the departing soul to heaven.

He has caused quarrels in our houses; riots in our cities, and murders within our borders.

He has peopled our alms-houses, jails and penitentiaries.

He has caused the mechanic to abandon his workshop, whilst his tools become broken and rusty.

He has caused the mariner to wreck his ship on the rocks of this world, and lose his soul on those of the next.

He has caused the laborer to neglect his hire, and the professional man his calling.

And, finally, destruction of every kind, is his ruling and preponderating tendency. He has cruelly outraged and oppressed every sex, age, rank, situation, and condition of life. Man has been hurled from his high estate, and glorious destiny. And lovely woman, driven from her angelic station,—the buoyant, blooming, and rich locked, youth,—the sedate and earnest man, of maturity,—the grey hairs of experience and the frosty head of age, have all been soiled, and crushed, under the foul tread of his brutal hoof.

But is there no antidote for all this bane? is there no balm in Gilead? There is, and it may be found in Total Abstinence!!

Then having armed our souls with courage and philanthropy, we will, not will, the end, and turn with repugnance from the means; but say, in the words of sobreness and truth, to all those who have abandoned the distilling and dealing in strong drinks, we embrace you from our hearts, as companions of our way. But those who still continue in the deep damnation of their odious calling, shall not swerve us from the path of duty. We will lift their ragged victims from the gutter, cleanse and clothe them in the habiliments of virtuous society, and raise their fallen spirits with the voice of encouragement and pity.

The reformed drunkard we will take by the hand, and treat him as a friend and a brother; visit his innocent family when the mists of the north are round the plain, and the snows of winter wreathe round their dwelling. His shivering children we will warm with the seraphic flame of charity; and the bruised and bleeding bosom of his wife, who has suffered alone and in silence, we will cover with the downy and glittering wings of hope; for yet, all may be well.

And if in the retrospective view of future ages, the generation which secured our civil liberty, under Washington, stands out in bold relief on the escutcheon of time, not less prominent will appear the present one, in which our moral independence will be achieved by the Washingtonians; for the fame of the patriot may be evanescent, but that of the philanthropist is permanent. In the first great struggle our fathers fell to the ground; but in this we rise from it. Then let us be true to our God,—true to ourselves,—and true to each other.

In conclusion, we will sip the dew-drop from the rose, and let the morning cup of bitters pass away; we will quench our noon-day thirst from the mossy bucket in the well, and crack the fiery bottle of intoxication; we will drink our evening beverage from the chrystal rill that oozes from the hill side, or out of the limpid brook of the valley, and dash to the earth the maddening bowl of rum, gin, or brandy. And, lastly, let us strive for progress in the sacred cause of temperance and virtue, and mutually cheer and assist each other through the thorny paths of this life; so that in the end, when we emerge on the distant plains of eternity we may be prepared to drink of those living waters, whose streams are benevolence, and mercy, and whose fountain is God.

And for the support of this declaration we will sign the pledge of Total Abstinence, and mutually pledge ourselves to support the cause of Temperance with our lives, our fortunes, and our sober honor

Engraved by Devereux & Brown, 116 Washington St., Boston.

Entered according to Act of Congress, by Charles Ellms.

Wm. White & H. F. Lewis, Printers, Spring Lane.

For more than half a century after 1776, the Declaration was primarily associated with secession and resistance to empire, rather than with the constitutional reform or revolutionary change within existing states. Neither the Declaration's proclamation of a right of rebellion against domestic tyranny nor its enumeration of the fundamental rights of individuals seemed self-evident or important to foreign observers or even to most Americans until after the War of 1812. To partisan opponents of Jefferson, to those who feared the backwash of the French Revolution and to those who wished to keep good relations with Great Britain, the Declaration remained a suspect and even dangerous document. The violence of the Haitian Revolution only confirmed such fears, and in 1804 Jefferson, as president, refused to recognize the black republic's declaration of independence—the first such anti-colonial declaration since 1776.

The United States generally looked more sympathetically on the Spanish-American independence movements of the 1810s and 1820s. Two American travelers in Chile and Mexico had distributed translations of the Declaration and the American Constitution "for the better promotion of the embryo cause" of their liberation, as one of them put it. During the course of the Spanish-American revolutions, multiple translations of the Declaration—"the true political decalogue," one translator called it—made their way to Colombia, Venezuela, and Ecuador.[6]

Among the fruits of these campaigns to disseminate the Declaration were the declarations of independence issued by almost all of the republics that emerged in Spanish America between 1810 (Colombia) and 1830 (Ecuador). The majority of these declarations followed the American model in stating their intention to become sovereign states. Thus, in 1811, Venezuela's representatives "declare[d] solemnly to the world, that these united Provinces are, and ought to be, from this day, by act and right, Free, Sovereign, and Independent States." Most did not enumerate rights and few listed grievances (which more often appeared in accompanying "manifestos"). This assertion of sovereignty and statehood would in fact be the Declaration's main legacy to world history in the nineteenth and twentieth centuries.

After the break-up of the Spanish overseas empire in Central and South America, the nineteenth century would witness remarkably few declarations of independence. Some continued the legacy of Spanish-American independence, in Texas (1836) or the Philippines (1898), but only one—the Liberian Declaration of Independence (1847)—was so deliberately modeled on the American example that it incorporated a statement of rights, as well as an announcement of statehood.

The seventy years before the First World War marked the high tide of empire across the world. In Europe, it was also a period in which claims to individual rights like those listed in the Declaration were less successful than those to corporate, collective, or group

OPPOSITE: *The success of the Declaration in securing American independence had the collateral effect of creating a new genre of expression that was adapted for other purposes. Leaders of the temperance movement used the Declaration as a model for expressing their quest to liberate families, communities, and workplaces from the tyranny of drunkenness.*

VOL. V.

NUMB. 256.

DUNLAP'S

Pennsylvania **Packet**

OR

GENERAL

THE

ADVERTISER.

TUESDAY, SEPTEMBER 17th, 1776.

rights that would define revolutionary ideologies like Socialism and Communism, as well as contemporary nationalist movements. The second half of the nineteenth century would thus be the low point in the Declaration's fortunes outside the United States.

CHARLESTOWN, *(South-Carolina)* *Aug.* 14. ON Monday laft week, the DECLARATION OF INDEPENDENCE was proclaimed here, amidft the acclamations of a vaft concourfe of people.

By letters of the 6th inftant from the Camp two miles below Keowee, in the Cherokee country, we have the following interefting intelligence:

On the 31ft of july, fome of Colonel Williamfon's fcouts took two white men prifoners, who had been fent to get cattle for the enemy. They informed the Colonel that Cameron had come over the Hills a few days before with twelve white men; and that he, with the Seneca and fome other Indians, in all about 150, were then encamped at Cowanarofs, about thirty miles from Twenty three Mile Creek, where our army then lay encamped; and that their women and children had all retired from the towns to the neighbourhood of the fame place. This intelligence determined the Colonel to march that evening at the head of 330 horfemen, taking the two prifoners with him. His intention was to leave the horfes two miles behind, with a party to guard them, and furround the enemy's camp by day break. The river Keowee lying in his route, and being only paffable at a ford at Seneca, obliged him to take that road. About one o'clock in the morning he arrived at the outfkirts of that town, which he had received accounts of being entirely abandoned; and therefore little expected to meet with any oppofition there. The enemy, however, having received fome intimation of his march, had taken poffeffion of the firft houfes, and pofted themfelves behind a long fence, ftuffed with twigs and corn blades, on an eminence clofe to the road where the party was to pafs; they allowed the guides and advanced guard to come almoft up to the houfes, when they fired five or fix guns, but without doing any other damage than killing one of the guide's horfes. They immediately afterwards began a very heavy fire on our advanced guard and main body; by which Mr. Francis Salvador was fhot in three different places, Colonel Williamfon had his horfe fhot under him, and eight men were badly wounded and two flightly. Mr. Salvador falling among the

The momentous character of Congress's decision, coupled with uncertain communications, meant that dissemination of the Declaration was itself news. Philadelphia publisher John Dunlap, who printed the first broadside of the Declaration, announced in the 17 September 1776 issue of his Pennsylvania Packet, or the General Advertiser the proclamation of the Declaration in Charleston, South Carolina, on 14 August. The fastest way information traveled between the two port cities was by coasting merchant ship, roughly a month-long journey.

Only in the aftermath of the First World War did the Declaration regain its global relevance. The great European land-empires of the Ottomans, the Romanovs, and the Habsburgs imploded just as challenges to European colonialism began to be heard from the Middle East to East Asia. Woodrow Wilson's powerful idea of self-determination—meaning both government by the consent of the governed internally and sovereign freedom from interference externally—inspired movements for autonomy across the world, many of whose leaders looked to the United States and its founding documents for inspiration.

Declarations of independence for Czechoslovakia, Korea, republican Ireland and Estonia, among others, all appeared within a few months of each other in 1918–19, especially leading up to and during the time of the Paris Peace Conference. In October 1918, the Czech nationalist Tomas Masaryk signed a "Declaration of Independence of the Mid-European Union" with a pen dipped in the inkwell in Independence Hall that had been used by the Declaration's signers. The following year, the First Korean Congress convened in Philadelphia in imitation of the Continental Congress to promote its own declaration of independence. The increasing prominence of America on the world scene spread the example of its history as a signal to others that they, too, could be liberated from empire. As the charter of that liberation, the Declaration became more widely known and more frequently imitated.

The Declaration reached its greatest prominence in world history in the half century after the Second World War. This was the result of two expansive sets of developments, the consequences of which fundamentally shaped the world we all inhabit today: the rise of rights talk around the world after 1945 and the process of decolonization that dissolved the European overseas empires. Human rights became a global language in this period and, though still far from universal, increasingly provided the means for subjects to make claims against their rulers and for the international community to judge the legitimacy of political regimes. Such judgments became more necessary with the rapid expansion of that community by the creation of new states from the wreckage of empire: more than half of the 192 states now represented at the United Nations emerged between 1945 and 1993, the majority with an announcement of statehood in the form of a declaration of independence. They ranged from the Republic of Vietnam—its declaration of independence in 1945 quoted the American Declaration in its opening lines—to the declarations that accompanied the exit of the former Soviet republics from the USSR and the dissolution of the federal republic of Yugoslavia. The greatest concentration of declarations of independence in world history came in 1990–93, as those two imperial structures collapsed. It is unlikely there ever again will be such a profusion of declarations, unless the United States or China—the world's two last great remaining land-empires—were to break up into a host of independent states or territories.

The Declaration of Independence came into its own as a global document in the last fifty years because it so precociously and succinctly stated conceptions of rights that have become increasingly relevant around the world, and because it provided the primary model for the declarations of independence on which so many contemporary states have been founded. Such widespread influence means that the Declaration may be even more

Declaring Independence in Vietnam

After decades of French colonial oppression and subsequent economic exploitation by the Japanese during World War II, Ho Chi Minh declared an independent Democratic Republic of Vietnam on 2 September 1945. His speech, delivered in Hanoi's Ba Dinh square before a crowd numbering more than half a million, was modeled upon and quoted the United States' Declaration of Independence:

"'All men are created equal. They are endowed by their Creator with certain inalienable rights, among these are Life, Liberty, and the pursuit of Happiness.'

"This immortal statement was made in the Declaration of Independence of the United States of America in 1776. In a broader sense, this means: All the peoples on the earth are equal from birth, all the peoples have a right to live, to be happy and free.

"The Declaration of the French Revolution made in 1791 on the Rights of Man and the Citizen also states: 'All men are born free and with equal rights, and must always remain free and have equal rights.' Those are undeniable truths.

"Nevertheless, for more than eighty years, the French imperialists, abusing the standard of Liberty, Equality, and Fraternity, have violated our Fatherland and oppressed our fellow-citizens. They have acted contrary to the ideals of humanity and justice. In the field of politics, they have deprived our people of every democratic liberty...."

[The closing lines of the speech:]

"We are convinced that the Allied nations which at Tehran and San Francisco have acknowledged the principles of self-determination and equality of nations, will not refuse to acknowledge the independence of Vietnam.

"A people who have courageously opposed French domination for more than eighty years, a people who have fought side by side with the Allies against the Fascists during these last years, such a people must be free and independent.

"For these reasons, we, members of the Provisional Government of the Democratic Republic of Vietnam, solemnly declare to the world that Vietnam has the right to be a free and independent country and in fact it is so already. The entire Vietnamese people are determined to mobilize all their physical and mental strength, to sacrifice their lives and property in order to safeguard their independence and liberty."

explosive today than it was in 1776. The mere possibility of a similar declaration from Taiwan could ignite a war between China and the United States. A hoax television report in December 2006 alleged Flanders had, once again, declared independence (this time from Belgium), provoking a national crisis. In Kosovo and Somalia, among other places around the world, declarations of independence await international recognition, while also attracting vehement opposition.

The document that introduced the United States among the powers of the earth and enabled other peoples to assert their independence has shaped our world in ways no other document of American history can match. How the Declaration of Independence might continue to shape our world is impossible to foretell. However, for the foreseeable future at least, it seems safe to predict that it will remain, as Jefferson thought it would, a document pregnant with the fate of America and the world.

Suggestions for Further Reading:

The main themes of this essay are developed at greater length in David Armitage, *The Declaration of Independence: A Global History* (Cambridge, MA, 2007), which includes the texts of many of the declarations of independence referred to here. More examples of declarations can be found in *Independence Documents of the World*, eds. Albert P. Blaustein, Jay Sigler, and Benjamin R. Beede, 2 vols. (New York, 1977). For treatments of the American Revolution in a wider global context, each of which touches on the Declaration's reception and influence, see Richard B. Morris, *The Emerging Nations and the American Revolution* (New York, 1970) and Erich Angermann, et al., *The Impact of the American Revolution Abroad* (Washington, DC, 1976). Peter S. Onuf, *Jefferson's Empire: The Language of Nationhood* (Charlottesville, 2000) treats Jefferson's conception of independence, and Lynn Hunt, *Inventing Human Rights: A History* (New York, 2007), places the Declaration in the broader history of eighteenth-century conceptions of rights. Erez Manela, *The Wilsonian Moment: Self-Determination and the International Origins of Anticolonial Nationalism* (New York, 2007), offers an excellent case study of the globalization of the ideals enshrined in the Declaration.

Notes

1 Jefferson to Roger C. Weightman, 24 June 1826, in *The Writings of Thomas Jefferson*, ed. Andrew A. Lipscomb and Albert Ellery Bergh, 20 vols. (Washington, DC, 1903–04), 16:181–82.

2 Abraham Lincoln, "Speech at Springfield, Illinois" (26 June 1857), in *The Collected Works of Abraham Lincoln*, ed. Roy P. Basler, 9 vols. (New Brunswick, NJ, 1953–55), 2:406.

3 Richard Henry Lee to Patrick Henry, 20 April 1776, in *The Letters of Richard Henry Lee*, ed. James Curtis Ballagh, 2 vols. (New York, 1911–14), 2:178.

4 Committee of Secret Correspondence to Silas Deane, 8 July 1776, in *Letters of Delegates to Congress, 1774–1789*, gen. ed. Paul H. Smith, 26 vols. to date (Washington, DC, 1976–), 4:405.

5 Abbé Genty, quoted in Daniel Mornet, *Les origines intellectuelles de la Révolution Française (1715–1787)*, 2nd edition, (Paris, 1934), 396–97.

6 Richard J. Cleveland, *A Narrative of Voyages and Commercial Enterprises*, 2 vols. (Cambridge, MA, 1842), 1:184; Vicente Rocafuerte, *Ideas necesarias á todo pueblo americano independiente, que quiera ser libre* (Philadelphia, 1821), 3.

Signers' Gallery

Signers of the Declaration

In the end, 56 delegates to the Second Continental Congress signed the Declaration. Of these, only 39 voted in favor of independence on 2 July 1776. One abstained, and one voted against it. Seven were away drafting state constitutions, leading militias, or otherwise absent. Eight were elected after the vote was taken. The New York delegation had been instructed to abstain from voting by New York's provincial congress, which only adopted independence on 9 July—five days after the Declaration had been approved and published. Still, it was enough to make the action unanimous and turn 13 formerly dependent British colonies into a new, united, and independent nation.

To memorialize the event, Congress ordered on 19 July that the text be "fairly engrossed on parchment, with the title and stile [sic] of 'The unanimous declaration of the thirteen United States of America,' and that the same, when engrossed, be signed by every member of Congress." Timothy Matlack, assistant to secretary Charles Thomson, probably performed the engrossing, or copying of the text in a large, clear hand. On 2 August, delegates gathered to ceremoniously affix their signatures to the document (now permanently displayed at the National Archives), beginning with John Hancock as president of Congress. Those who were absent added their names later, including Matthew Thornton, who did not find room to sign by his fellow New Hampshire delegates, and Thomas McKean of Delaware, who was the last to sign, sometime in early 1777.

Two well-known historic paintings are commonly thought to represent the signing, but in fact commemorate the presentation of the draft Declaration to Congress on 28 June. The more famous image by John Trumbull (1756–1843) was engraved and popularly reprinted (see timeline on p. xv). The preceding page reproduces a painting begun by Robert Edge Pine (ca. 1730–88) that was later completed by Edward Savage (1761–1817). The series of 49 signers' portraits shown in the following gallery closely resemble the figures in Pine's painting; portraits of the remaining signers are reproduced from other sources.

John Adams
Massachusetts
1735–1826

The "Atlas of Independence," John Adams was schooled in Braintree, Massachusetts, and then Harvard. Forsaking ministry for law, he gained notoriety in 1765 for essays rousing citizens from "sordid ignorance" and attacking Britain's Parliament for divesting colonists of "essential rights and liberties." He famously defended clients ranging from smuggler John Hancock to British soldiers accused in the Boston Massacre. Adams was elected to the Massachusetts Assembly in 1770, which sent him to the Continental Congress in 1774, where he served energetically on 90 committees, including one to draft the Declaration of Independence. Though a vigorous essayist and political theorist, he deferred drafting the Declaration to Virginia's Thomas Jefferson, recognizing his eloquence and being mindful to deemphasize New England's role. In the debates over independence, Jefferson characterized Adams as "our *Colossus* on the floor." Beginning in 1778, Congress sent Adams on a series of diplomatic missions to Europe to secure aid from France and Holland, and then to achieve peace with Britain. In 1788 and 1792, he was elected vice president as a Federalist and in 1796, president by a slight margin over Jefferson, who became his vice president. Tensions with France, repression at home, and a split in Federalist ranks contributed to his loss of the presidency to Jefferson in 1800. In retirement, Adams and Jefferson reconciled and sustained an extraordinary correspondence until their deaths within hours of each other on the 50th anniversary of Independence.

Samuel Adams
Massachusetts
1722–1803

Architect of resistance to Britain, Samuel Adams was the son of a Boston merchant and brewer and second cousin to John Adams. His two Harvard degrees included a 1743 master's defense of the Lockean thesis that democracies were entitled to revolt against tyranny once all peaceful means of redress failed. Ill-suited for ministry, a failure in business, and an inefficient tax collector, Adams had a consuming thirst for politics. Publishing essays defending the rights and liberties of mankind as early as 1748, he rose to lead Boston's influential South End caucus. In the wake of 1765 Stamp Act riots, Adams was elected to the Massachusetts legislature. A powerful orator and writer, Adams rejected claims of unlimited parliamentary power over colonial assemblies. Ever an agitator, he led the "Sons of Liberty," stirred effective boycotts of British commerce, organized intercolonial committees of correspondence, orchestrated the Boston Tea Party, and proposed formation of a Continental Congress, which he served passionately from 1774 to 1781. Known variously as the "father," "grand incendiary," or "firebrand" of the American Revolution, his role lay more in undermining the old order than in crafting the new. "The last of the Puritans," Adams took pride in his poverty; even his foes testified to his incorruptibility. In 1788, he played a crucial role in Massachusetts's provisional ratification of the federal Constitution, and later served as governor from 1794 to 1797.

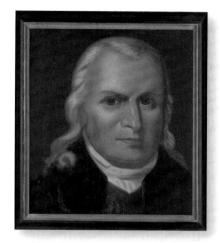

Charles Carroll

Maryland
1737–1832

Among Declaration signers, Charles Carroll of Carrollton was the richest, the only Roman Catholic, and the last to die. Son of a wealthy Maryland planter, Carroll studied for 18 years in France and England. In 1773, under the pseudonym "First Citizen," he published influential essays criticizing the governor's unilateral fee increases for public services. Cracking a ban against Catholics holding office, he was appointed to Maryland's first council of safety in 1774 and its provincial congress. He helped turn Maryland's vote for independence and was elected to Congress on 4 July 1776. Too late to vote for the Declaration, Carroll signed it on 2 August. Toward the end of his life, he reflected that he had "zealously" supported the revolution to "obtain religious as well as civil liberty." Carroll served in the Maryland Senate from 1781 to 1800, including three years in the U.S. Senate (1789–92). An aristocratic Federalist, he was alarmed by egalitarian forces unleashed by the American and French revolutions. He publicly called slavery an evil, but emancipated only one of his more than 300 slaves upon his death. In 1830, he served as president of the American Colonization Society, which founded Liberia. With the deaths of John Adams and Thomas Jefferson in 1826, Carroll became the sole surviving signer of the Declaration, inspiring Daniel Webster to venerate him as "an aged oak, standing alone on the plain."

Samuel Chase

Maryland
1741–1811

Known as Maryland's Demosthenes, Samuel Chase was tutored in the classics by his father, the Anglican rector of Baltimore. Following two years of legal study, he was admitted to the bar at age 20. In 1764, he was elected to Maryland's legislature. Admired for his fervent eloquence on behalf of colonial rights, he was sent as a delegate to the First Continental Congress in 1774. In that role, Chase took part in a failed mission to persuade Canada to join the resistance to Britain. In late June 1776, he orchestrated a campaign in the Maryland Assembly to reverse its loyalist stance and authorize its congressional delegates to vote for independence. In 1787, he voted with the antifederalists against the new Constitution during Maryland's ratifying convention. The next year, Chase began a judicial career, rising to chief judge in Maryland's General Court. By the time he was appointed an associate justice of the U.S. Supreme Court in 1795, he had switched camps, becoming an ardent Federalist. His opinions helped lay the foundations for judicial review of legislative actions. Ironically, Chase was impeached by Congress in 1804 for misconduct in high profile treason and sedition cases. However, a dramatic Senate trial acquitted him, due to a split over the definition of "high crimes and misdemeanors." Chase remained on the high court until his death in 1811.

Josiah Bartlett (1729–1795)

NEW HAMPSHIRE. Respected physician, legislator, and militia colonel, Bartlett sided early with revolutionary sentiment. He was the first to sign the engrossed Declaration after John Hancock and supported construction of America's first navy ships. After the war, he served a decade as a justice, then four years as chief executive of New Hampshire.

Carter Braxton (1736–1797)

VIRGINIA. Wealthy merchant and plantation owner, Braxton sympathized with colonial grievances against Britain while holding out hope for reconciliation. After signing the Declaration, he lost his congressional seat over his conservative proposals for Virginia's constitution. He subsequently served eight terms in Virginia's House of Delegates. Substantial shipping losses during the war and later commercial failures diminished his fortune.

Abraham Clark (1726–1794)

NEW JERSEY. Self-educated surveyor and "poor man's lawyer," Clark was sent to Congress in June 1776 to support a stronger New Jersey stance for independence. In subsequent state and national legislative service, he was noted for advocating paper money credit and opposing special privileges for lawyers and military officers.

George Clymer (1739–1813)

PENNSYLVANIA. A wealthy Philadelphia merchant and early agitator for independence, Clymer was appointed to Congress in time to sign the Declaration. He also served on the committees war and treasury. An advocate for federal taxation, Clymer's tenure as supervisor of revenues for Pennsylvania ended during the 1794 Whiskey Rebellion. Later known for philanthropy, he served as president of the Pennsylvania Academy of Fine Arts.

William Ellery (1727–1820)

RHODE ISLAND. Harvard-educated, Ellery became a wealthy merchant, tax collector, and lawyer. During a decade of service to Congress, he focused on maritime affairs. British forces destroyed his Newport home in 1778. A noted abolitionist, President Washington appointed him customs collector for Newport in 1790, a post he held for 30 years, until his death at 92.

William Floyd (1734–1821)

NEW YORK. Planter, militia officer, and Suffolk County Delegate to the Continental Congress, Floyd was the first New Yorker to sign the Declaration. When British forces occupied Long Island, Floyd's family fled to Connecticut. He remained active in national politics and spent the last 18 years of his long life farming in upstate New York.

Button Gwinnett (1735–1777)

GEORGIA. Born in England, Gwinnett came to Georgia as a young merchant. Unsuccessful in mercantile and plantation ventures, he gained prominence as a rural patriot activist, and was sent to Congress in 1776. After helping to write a new Georgia constitution, he commanded the state's militia on a failed invasion of Florida. A political rival killed him in a duel in May 1777.

Lyman Hall (1724–1790)

GEORGIA. Minister, physician, and planter, Hall was raised in Connecticut and graduated from Yale. He migrated to Georgia, where he helped organize patriot resistance. In 1778, British forces occupied Georgia and burned Hall's plantation. After the war, Hall became governor and helped charter the University of Georgia.

Benjamin Harrison (1726–1791)

VIRGINIA. A wealthy planter, Harrison long served in Virginia's House of Burgesses. Although resistant to war and Virginia radicals in Congress, he endorsed independence and was chosen to chair the debates over the Declaration and announced its approval. He later served as Virginia's speaker of the house and governor. His son and great-grandson became U.S. presidents.

John Hart (1714–1779)

NEW JERSEY. A prosperous farmer, miller, judge, and legislator, Hart went to Congress in June 1776. After voting for independence and signing the Declaration on 2 August, he returned to New Jersey's lower house and was appointed speaker. In November, British troops forced him into hiding and looted his Hopewell farm. He returned and died three years later from kidney stones.

Joseph Hewes (1730–1779)

NORTH CAROLINA. Educated at the College of New Jersey (now Princeton), Hewes made his fortune in shipping in North Carolina. Hewes resisted independence until 1 July when, according to John Adams, he cried out, "It is done! I will abide by it." Committed to the cause, Hewes rented his ships to Congress, but insisted on payment in gold rather than inflated continental currency.

Thomas Heyward (1746–1809)

SOUTH CAROLINA. Wealthy planter, London-trained lawyer, Heyward served as a judge, legislator, and military officer in his native South Carolina. Initially a moderate, in Congress he supported independence. A militia captain in the defense of Charleston in 1780, he was captured and held prisoner for over a year. Later in life, he became a noted agricultural pioneer.

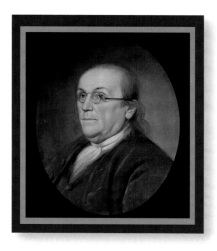

Benjamin Franklin

Pennsylvania
1706–1790

Publisher, scientist, diplomat, philosopher, civic activist, Benjamin Franklin was the Revolution's elder statesman. Youngest son to a Boston candlemaker's 13 children, Franklin learned printing, satire, and the perils of dissent as apprentice to his brother James. His own successful Philadelphia printing business featured the *Pennsylvania Gazette* and *Poor Richard's Almanac*, which made him famous for his satirical wit, wisdom, and citizen advocacy. Largely self-educated, Franklin won international acclaim for scientific discoveries and inventions, including the lightning rod, the "Franklin" Stove, and bifocals. Franklin was also a civic pioneer in organizing a public library, a militia, a hospital, a learned society, fire and insurance companies, and what became the University of Pennsylvania. In 1751, he was elected to the Pennsylvania Assembly, which sent him to Britain to explain American grievances. His writings galvanized the Revolution. His 1775 hoax, "Bradshaw's Epitaph," provided Thomas Jefferson with his personal motto: "rebellion to tyrants is obedience to God." A delegate to the Continental Congress, he aided Jefferson as a member of the committee charged with drafting the Declaration of Independence. From 1776 to 1785, Franklin served as America's master diplomat to France, where his celebrity status and brilliant propaganda efforts earned France's critical aid for the American cause. At the 1787 Constitutional Convention, his harmonizing presence and advocacy of compromises ensured its success. Franklin continued his activism, especially on behalf of Indians and against slavery, until his death in 1790.

Elbridge Gerry

Massachusetts
1744–1814

The brightest of 12 children of a successful merchant, Elbridge Gerry earned two Harvard degrees. His 1765 master's thesis advocated evasion of Stamp Act duties. Following the Boston Massacre in 1770, Gerry helped orchestrate the boycott of the Townshend Acts and later aided Sam Adams with the vital "committees of correspondence" to rally opposition. Gerry's merchant skills were deployed to secure military supplies, first in Massachusetts and then nationally, upon being sent to the Second Continental Congress. Of his actions there, John Adams wrote: "If every man here was a Gerry, the Liberties of America would be safe against the Gates of Earth and Hell." Shay's Rebellion stirred Gerry to an active, compromiser role in the 1787 Constitutional Convention, even as he refused to sign it without a Bill of Rights. One of several envoys to France in 1797, he endured the insults of the "XYZ Affair" and averted war. Gerry's unintended legacy stems from actions as Massachusetts governor in 1811. Fearing Federalists were pursuing reunion with Britain, Gerry invoked an old practice to engineer electoral dilution of Federalist strength by concentrating them in fewer districts. One resulting district, shaped like a salamander, was dubbed "gerrymandered"— thus the term. In 1812, Gerry was elected vice president to James Madison. He died in office two years later.

John Hancock

Massachusetts
1737–1793

Fatherless at age seven, John Hancock was raised by a merchant uncle who financed his studies at Boston Latin School and Harvard. While learning his uncle's businesses, he visited Britain, where he witnessed George III's coronation. He inherited his uncle's financial empire in 1764, just as the Sugar and Stamp Acts threatened business. Hancock's ascent in revolutionary politics was aided by his influence as one of Boston's largest employers and creditors. In 1768, his sloop *Liberty* was impounded for smuggling, a seizure characterized as British tyranny. Violently confronted by the "Sons of Liberty," the customs officials fled, rendering Hancock a patriot legend. When Britain clamped down on Boston after the Tea Party, Hancock was elected president of the provincial congress, which sent him to the Continental Congress. Avoiding capture at Lexington in April 1775, thanks to warnings from Paul Revere, Hancock was subsequently elected president of the Continental Congress, a role he relished with great pomp. Famous for being the first to sign the Declaration with his flamboyant signature, his extravagant style nevertheless annoyed many in Congress. Unfazed, Hancock returned to Massachusetts to be elected in 1780 as the commonwealth's first governor. In January 1788, he turned a closely divided Massachusetts convention in favor of the federal Constitution. Hancock's sustained populist appeal was evident in his repeated re-elections until his death in 1793.

William Hooper (1742–1790)

NORTH CAROLINA. Reputed "Prophet of Independence," Hooper, a Boston-educated lawyer, helped smash the "regulator" rebellion at the 1771 Battle of Alamance. Turning against North Carolina's royal governor, he predicted in April 1774, "The Colonies are striding fast to independence." A delegate to Congress from 1774 to 1777, he was noted as one of its best orators. In 1781, Hooper's home was wrecked by British troops.

Samuel Huntington (1731–1796)

CONNECTICUT. A largely self-educated lawyer, Huntington served intermittently in Congress from 1775–1784, including two years as its president during the adoption of the Articles of Confederation. The last 10 years of his life, he served as a popular Connecticut governor.

Francis Lightfoot Lee (1734–1797)

VIRGINIA. From a prominent Virginia planter family, Lee was a noted radical in the House of Burgesses in the decade leading up to the Revolution. He served in Congress from 1775 to 1779. Unlike his more famous older brother, Richard Henry, Francis supported ratification of the Constitution in 1787.

Stephen Hopkins

Rhode Island
1707–1785

A self-educated farmer's son, Stephen Hopkins prospered in surveying, shipbuilding, publishing, trading, and iron smelting. His long public service began in 1731, in Scituate, Rhode Island, as clerk, solicitor, council president, and justice of the peace. From 1744 to 1754, and again from 1771 to 1776, he was elected to Rhode Island's General Assembly, where he rose to serve simultaneously as speaker and justice. In between, he was elected to serve nine one-year terms as governor. In 1754, as a delegate to the Albany convention, he supported Benjamin Franklin's plan for colonial union. In 1764, Hopkins was appointed the first chancellor of what became Brown University. The same year, he became famous for penning two pamphlets, the first explaining how the Sugar Act would affect colonial trade. The second, *The Rights of the Colonies Examined*, posited that colonial affairs and taxes were best administered by local assemblies. In 1772, as chief justice of the Rhode Island Superior Court, Hopkins blocked British efforts to detain citizens accused of burning the British revenue schooner H.M.S. *Gaspee*. As a delegate to the Continental Congresses, he played a key role in creating the Continental Navy and helped draft the Articles of Confederation. At age 69 and afflicted with palsy, Hopkins reputedly declared upon signing the Declaration of Independence, "My hand trembles, but my heart does not!" He withdrew from national service soon after.

Francis Hopkinson

New Jersey
1737–1791

Satirist, composer, merchant, artist, and judge, Francis Hopkinson served the patriot cause most with his poetry, prose, and music. Among the first graduates of the College of Philadelphia, he pursued a career in property law and commerce. During a visit to England, he sought customs appointments from top Crown officials. By 1773, as his Philadelphia import business declined, he moved to his wife's hometown of Bordenton, New Jersey. Hopkinson's growing sympathies for the patriot cause found voice through his established talents as a poet and musician. "A Pretty Story" (1774) was a popular spoof of British colonial attitudes. Among his best known Revolutionary ballads and essays, "A Prophecy" (1776) anticipated independence; "The Birds, the Beasts, and the Bat" (1778) ridiculed fence-sitters; and "The Battle of the Kegs" (1778) famously lampooned the alarm caused by crude patriot mines on the Delaware River. Skilled as a draftsman, he designed emblems for coins and currency and government seals. Apart from his artistic endeavors, Hopkinson fulfilled various roles as a public servant, including customs collector. He voted for independence as a New Jersey delegate to the Second Continental Congress, where he served from 1776 to 1778, resigning to take charge of the Continental Loan Office. From 1779 to 1789, he was a judge on Pennsylvania's Admiralty Court, and, from 1790 until his death, a U.S. district judge for Pennsylvania.

Thomas Jefferson

Virginia
1743–1826

Primary author of the Declaration of Independence, Thomas Jefferson gave voice to America's fundamental principles and aspirations. Son of a prominent landholder, he was tutored in the classics, attended the College of William and Mary, and studied law with George Wythe. At 23, he was elected to Virginia's House of Burgesses. In 1774, he wrote the widely circulated pamphlet *Summary View of the Rights of British America*. Sent to the Second Continental Congress in 1775, his "peculiar felicity of expression" was deployed in drafting the Declaration of Independence. Returning to Virginia, Jefferson's legal reform proposals included what became the seminal Statute on Religious Freedom, which his friend James Madison guided through Virginia's legislature in 1786. Jefferson's brief terms as governor and congressman were followed by service as ambassador to France, secretary of state, vice president, and president. As president, he struggled to preserve America's independence while avoiding "entangling alliances" and doubling its size with the Louisiana Purchase. In personal pursuits, Jefferson excelled as an architect, agronomist, scientist, musician, inventor, and author. His one book, *Notes on the State of Virginia*, a discourse on natural and political systems, was occasioned by questions from a French diplomat. A notable book collector, Jefferson sold his personal library to the nation after the British burned the original Library of Congress during the War of 1812. Jefferson devoted his final years to his Monticello plantation and founding the University of Virginia.

Richard Henry Lee

Virginia
1733–1794

Born to a prominent Virginia planter family, Richard Henry Lee was schooled at Wakefield Academy in Yorkshire, England. At 26 he was appointed justice of the peace in Westmoreland County and then elected to the Virginia House of Burgesses. When the Stamp Act taxes were announced, Lee initially applied to collect the levies, but soon began leading protests against them. As colonial discontent grew, Lee helped organize intercolonial correspondence committees, and he was among the Virginia radicals who convened at the Raleigh Tavern after the royal governor dissolved the Burgesses. Lee was elected to the First Continental Congress, where he gained fame as an "American Cicero" for orations that matched Patrick Henry's in their force and for his work on a Declaration of Rights. Lee's three famous resolutions of 7 June 1776 proposed American independence, an alliance with France, and a plan of interstate confederation. When war came to Virginia, Lee proposed that George Washington be given dictatorial powers. Yet after the war, Lee's antifederalist views inclined him to fear centralized power, and he opposed the 1787 Constitution. The subsequent Bill of Rights did not mollify his concerns about a "tendency to consolidated Empire." Lee served one Senate term in the new federal government before retiring from public life in 1792.

Thomas McKean

Delaware
1734–1817

Born in Chester County, Pennsylvania, to Scotch-Irish immigrants, Thomas McKean studied at Francis Allison's New London Academy. At 16, he went to New Castle, Delaware, to study law. Admitted to the bar at 20, he soon established a pattern of simultaneously serving multiple offices in Delaware, Pennsylvania, and New Jersey, often while holding national posts. Rising to speaker of the Delaware Assembly in 1772, he represented Delaware at the Continental Congress from 1774 to 1783. When McKean discovered on 1 July 1776 that Delaware's independence vote was split, he urgently summoned Caesar Rodney, who arrived the next day to cast Delaware's deciding vote for independence. McKean was the last to sign the Declaration, probably in early 1777, as he was away serving as a colonel—in New Jersey's militia. In 1777, McKean was appointed chief justice of Pennsylvania, where over a 22-year career, he established the state's high court as a formidable, independent, and moderating institution, striking down legislative acts deemed unconstitutional a decade before *Marbury v. Madison*. During the latter half of 1781, he was the first "President of the United States in Congress Assembled" elected under a ratified Articles of Confederation. As Pennsylvania's governor in 1799, McKean introduced the "spoils system," replacing Federalist civil servants with Republicans, who later opposed him.

The Congress of Independence

Represented	Name	Birthplace	Vote on Independence	Signer?
Connecticut	**Samuel Huntington** (1731–1796)	Windham, Connecticut	For	Yes
Connecticut	**Roger Sherman** (1721–1793)	Newtown, Massachusetts	For*	Yes
Connecticut	**William Williams** (1731–1811)	New London, Connecticut	Not in Congress (arrived 7/28/1776)	Yes
Connecticut	**Oliver Wolcott** (1726–1797)	Windsor, Connecticut	Absent	Yes
Delaware	**Thomas McKean** (1734–1817)	New London Township, Pennsylvania	For	Yes
Delaware	**George Read** (1733–1798)	Cecil County, Maryland	Against	Yes
Delaware	**Caesar Rodney** (1728–1784)	Kent County, near Dover, Delaware	For	Yes
Georgia	**Button Gwinnett** (1735–1777)	Gloucestershire, England	For	Yes
Georgia	**Lyman Hall** (1724–1790)	Wallingford, Connecticut	For	Yes
Georgia	**George Walton** (1749?–1804)	Farmville, Virginia	For	Yes
Maryland	**Charles Carroll of Carrollton** (1737–1832)	Annapolis, Maryland	Not in Congress (elected 7/4/1776)	Yes
Maryland	**Samuel Chase** (1741–1811)	Somerset County, Maryland	For	Yes
Maryland	**William Paca** (1740–1799)	Near Abingdon, Baltimore County, Maryland	For	Yes
Maryland	**Thomas Stone** (1743–1787)	Charles County, Marlyand	For	Yes
Massachusetts	**John Adams** (1735–1826)	Braintree (now Quincy), Massachusetts	For*	Yes
Massachusetts	**Samuel Adams** (1722–1803)	Boston, Massachusetts	For	Yes
Massachusetts	**Elbridge Gerry** (1744–1814)	Marblehead, Massachusetts	For	Yes
Massachusetts	**John Hancock** (1737–1793)	Braintree (now Quincy), Massachusetts	For	Yes
Massachusetts	**Robert Treat Paine** (1731–1814)	Boston, Massachusetts	For	Yes
New Hampshire	**Josiah Bartlett** (1729–1795)	Amesbury, Massachusetts	For	Yes
New Hampshire	**Matthew Thornton** (1714?–1803)	Ireland	Not in Congress (appointed 9/1776)	Yes
New Hampshire	**William Whipple** (1730–1785)	Kittery, Massachusetts (now Maine)	For	Yes
New Jersey	**Abraham Clark** (1726–1794)	Elizabeth, New Jersey	For	Yes
New Jersey	**John Hart** (1714–1779)	Stonington, Connecticut	For	Yes
New Jersey	**Francis Hopkinson** (1737–1791)	Philadelphia, Pennsylvania	For	Yes
New Jersey	**Richard Stockton** (1730–1781)	Princeton, New Jersey	For	Yes
New Jersey	**John Witherspoon** (1723–1794)	Gifford, Scotland	For	Yes
New York	**George Clinton** (1739–1812)	Ulster (now Orange) County, New York	Absent	No
New York	**William Floyd** (1734–1821)	Mastic, Long Island, New York	Abstained by instruction†	Yes
New York	**Francis Lewis** (1713–1802)	Llandaff, Glamorganshire, Wales	Abstained by instruction†	Yes
New York	**Philip Livingston** (1716–1778)	Albany, New York	Absent	Yes
New York	**Robert Livingston** (1746–1813)	New York, New York	Abstained by instruction†	No

Notes: * Served on the committee to draft the Declaration of Independence in June 1776.
    † The New York Provincial Congress instructed its delegates to abstain from voting on independence while the matter was being debated in Philadelphia. Following the adoption of the Declaration on 4 July, New York approved a resolution endorsing independence on 9 July.

Education	Public Offices
Limited schooling; cooper's apprentice; read law with Colonel Jedidiah Elderkin	Assemblyman; Royal Councilor for Connecticut; President of the United States in Congress Assembled; Chief Justice, Superior Court; Lieutenant Governor; Governor
Attended district schools; tutored by Rev. Samuel Danbar	Assemblyman; Justice of the Peace; Judge, County and Superior Courts; Treasurer, Yale; Connecticut Council of Safety; Delegate to the Constitutional Convention
Harvard	State Assemblyman and Speaker; Governor's Council; Judge, County and Probate Courts; Delegate, Connecticut Convention to ratify the U.S. Constitution
Yale; medical studies with uncle Alexander Wolcott	Sheriff, Litchfield; Judge, Probate and County Courts; Indian Commissioner; Governor
Rev. Francis Alison's New London Academy; read law with cousin David Finney	Chief Justice (Pennsylvania); Governor (Pennsylvania); Assemblyman (Delaware); Judge, County Court (Delaware); President of the United States in Congress Assembled
Rev. Francis Alison's New London Academy; read law with John Moland	Attorney General for the Lower Counties (Delaware); Delegate, Delaware Constitutional Convention; Judge, Admiralty Court of the Confederation; Chief Justice, Delaware Supreme Court
Unknown	Sheriff, Kent County; Justice of the Peace; Clerk, Judge, Orphans and County Courts; Supreme Court Justice, Lower Counties (Delaware); Assemblyman (Speaker); President of Delaware
Unknown	Assemblyman; Justice of the Peace; President, Council of Safety
Yale; studied theology with uncle Samuel Hall; medical apprenticeship	Assemblyman; Judge; Governor
Self-educated; carpenter's apprentice; read law with Henry Young	President, Council of Safety; Governor; Justice, Chief Justice, Georgia Supreme Court; U.S. Senator
College of St. Omer; Jesuit Seminary in Rheims, France; College of Louis de Grand; law studies at Bourges and Inner Temple, London	Committees of Correspondence and Safety; State Senator; United States Senator
Home-schooled in the classics; read law at Hammond & Hall, Annapolis	Assemblyman; Committee of Correspondence; Chief Justice, Criminal Court; Chief Judge, General Court; Delegate, Maryland Convention to ratify the U.S. Constitution; Justice, Supreme Court of the United States
Private tutoring; College of Philadelphia; read law in the office of Stephen Bordley; law studies at Inner Temple, London	Assemblyman; Committee of Correspondence; Chief Judge, General Court; Chief Justice, Confederation Court of Appeals; Governor; Delegate, Maryland Convention to ratify the U.S. Constitution; U.S. District Judge for Maryland
Scottish tutor[?]; read law with Thomas Johnson	Committee of Correspondence; State Senator; U.S. Congressman
Home-schooled; Dame Belcher's School; Joseph Cleverly's Latin School; Harvard; read law with James Putnam	Confederation Minister to France and Great Britain; Vice President of the U.S.; President of the U.S.
Boston Latin School; Harvard; countinghouse apprentice	Colonial Tax Collector; Assemblyman; Delegate, Massachusetts Convention to ratify the U.S. Constitution; Lieutenant Governor; Governor
Harvard; countinghouse apprentice	Committees of Correspondence and Safety; Assemblyman; Representative, General Court; Confederation Congressman; Delegate, U.S. Constitutional Convention; Envoy to France; Vice President of the U.S.; Governor
Boston Latin School; Harvard; countinghouse apprentice	Committee of Safety; Assemblyman (Speaker); Executive Council; President of the United States in Congress Assembled; Governor
Boston Latin School; Harvard College; read law with Benjamin Pratt	Justice of the Peace; Assemblyman; Attorney General; Executive Council; Justice, Supreme Judicial Court
Circuit schools; privately tutored in the classics by Rev. John Webster; Studied medicine with James Ordway	Town Selectman; Assemblyman; Justice of the Peace; Delegate, U.S. Constitutional Convention; Judge, Court of Common Pleas; Chief Justice; Chief Executive/Governor
Unknown	Assemblyman (Speaker); Judge, Superior Court; Committee of Safety
Public school; privately tutored by Robert Elliot Gerish	Assemblyman; Committee of Safety; Justice, New Hampshire Supreme Court; Justice of the Peace
Some public schooling	Committee of Safety; Assemblyman; Delegate, Annapolis Convention; U.S. Congressman
Unknown	Assemblyman; Judge, Court of Common Pleas; Town Alderman; Committees of Safety and Correspondence
College of Philadelphia	Customs Inspector; Judge, Admiralty Court; Judge, U.S. District Court
Samuel Finley's Academy, West Nottingham, Maryland; studied law with David Ogden	Justice, Supreme Court (New Jersey); Executive Council
Haddington Grammer School; University of Edinburgh; University of St. Andrews[?]	Confederation Congressman; State Legislator; Delegate, New Jersey Convention to ratify the U.S. Constitution
Law studies	Clerk, District Attorney, Court of Common Pleas; Assemblyman; Committee of Correspondence; Governor; President, New York Convention to ratify the U.S. Consitition; Vice President of the U.S.
Private tutoring[?]	Assemblyman; Delegate, New York Convention to ratify the U.S. Consitition; U.S. Congressman
Westminster School, London; countinghouse apprentice	Committee of Correspondence
Yale College	City Alderman; Assemblyman (Speaker); Committee of Correspondence
King's College (Columbia); law studies with cousin William Livingston	Assemblyman; Delegate, New York Constitutional Convention; Confederation Secretary of Foreign Affairs; Chancellor of New York; U.S. Minister to France

The Congress of Independence

Represented	Name	Birthplace	Vote on Independence	Signer?
New York	Lewis Morris (1726–1798)	New York, New York	Absent	Yes
North Carolina	Joseph Hewes (1730–1779)	Kingston, New Jersey	For	Yes
North Carolina	William Hooper (1742–1790)	Boston, Massachusetts	Absent	Yes
North Carolina	John Penn (1740–1788)	Caroline County, Virginia	For	Yes
Pennsylvania	George Clymer (1739–1813)	Philadelphia, Pennsylvania	Not in Congress‡	Yes
Pennsylvania	John Dickinson (1732–1808)	Talbot County, Maryland	Abstained	No
Pennsylvania	Benjamin Franklin (1706–1790)	Boston, Massachusetts	For*	Yes
Pennsylvania	Charles Humphreys (1714–1786)	Haverford, Pennsylvania	Against	No
Pennsylvania	Robert Morris (1735–1806)	Liverpool, England	Abstained	Yes
Pennsylvania	John Morton (1725–1777)	Ridley Township, Pennsylvania	For	Yes
Pennsylvania	George Ross (1730–1779)	New Castle, Delaware	Not in Congress‡	Yes
Pennsylvania	Benjamin Rush (1746–1813)	near Philadelphia, Pennsylvania	Not in Congress‡	Yes
Pennsylvania	James Smith (1719–1806)	northern Ireland	Not in Congress‡	Yes
Pennsylvania	George Taylor (1716–1781)	Antrim, northern Ireland	Not in Congress‡	Yes
Pennsylvania	Charles Thomson (1729–1824)	Maghera (Londonderry), Ireland	Not a voting member (Secretary)	No
Pennsylvania	James Wilson (1742–1798)	Carskerdo, St. Andrews, Scotland	For	Yes
Pennsylvania	Thomas Willing (1731–1821)	Philadelphia, Pennsylvania	Against	No
Rhode Island	William Ellery (1727–1820)	Newport, Rhode Island	For	Yes
Rhode Island	Stephen Hopkins (1707–1785)	Providence, Rhode Island	For	Yes
South Carolina	Thomas Heyward (1746–1809)	St. Helen's Parish (Jasper County), Georgia	For	Yes
South Carolina	Thomas Lynch, Jr. (1749–1779)	Winyaw, South Carolina	For	Yes
South Carolina	Arthur Middleton (1742–1787)	Charlestown (now Charleston), South Carolina	For	Yes
South Carolina	Edward Rutledge (1749–1800)	Christ Church Parish, South Carolina	For	Yes
Virginia	Carter Braxton (1736–1797)	Newington, Virginia	For	Yes
Virginia	Benjamin Harrison (1726–1791)	Charles City County, Virginia	For	Yes
Virginia	Thomas Jefferson (1743–1826)	Goochland (now Albemarle) County, Virginia	For*	Yes
Virginia	Richard Henry Lee (1733–1794)	Westmoreland County, Virginia	For	Yes
Virginia	Francis Lightfoot Lee (1734–1797)	Westmoreland County, Virginia	For	Yes
Virginia	Thomas Nelson (1738–1789)	Yorktown, Virginia	For	Yes
Virginia	George Wythe (1726?–1806)	Elizabeth City County, Virginia	Absent	Yes

Notes: * Served on the committee to draft the Declaration of Independence in June 1776.
‡ Appointed 7/20/1776 by Pennsylvania's constitutional convention.

Education	Public Offices
Attended Yale	Indian Commissioner; Judge, County Court; Assemblyman; Delegate, New York Convention to ratify the U.S. Constitution
Classical education; College of New Jersey (Princeton)	Assemblyman/Provincial Congressman; Committee of Correspondence
Boston Latin School; Harvard College; studied law with George Otis	Assemblyman/Provincial Congressman; Deputy Attorney General; Committee of Correspondence
Some public schooling; studied law with uncle Edmund Pendleton	Assemblyman/Provincial Congressman; Confederation Receiver of Taxes for North Carolina; North Carolina Board of War; Governor's Council
Schooling unknown; apprentice in uncle's countinghouse	Council of Safety; Indian Commissioner; Confederation Congressman; State Legislator; Delegate, U.S. Constitutional Convention; U.S. Supervisor of Revenue for Pennsylvania; U.S. Congressman
Private tutoring; law studies at Middle Temple, London	Assemblyman, Lower Counties (Delaware); Assemblyman (Pennsylvania); President, State of Delaware; President, Pennsylvania; Delegate, U.S. Constitutional Convention (from Delaware)
Boston Latin School; George Brownell's English School	Colonial Agent in London for Pennsylvania, Georgia, New Jersey, and Massachusetts; Continental Congress Postmaster General; Minister to France; President, Pennsylvania Executive Council; Delegate, U.S. Constitutional Convention
Unknown	Assemblyman
Unknown; apprentice to merchant Charles Willing	Committees of Safety and Correspondence; Assemblyman; Confederation Superintendent of Finance
Home-schooled; studied surveying and law with his stepfather	Justice of the Peace; County Sheriff; Assemblyman (Speaker); Judge, Courts of General Sessions and Common Pleas
Home-schooled; studied law with stepbrother John Ross	Assemblyman; Committee of Safety; Indian Commissioner; Delegate, Pennsylvania Constitutional Convention; Judge, Admiralty Court
Samuel Finley's Academy, Nottingham, Maryland; College of New Jersey (Princeton); studied medicine with John Redman; College of Philadelphia; University of Edinburgh; St. Thomas Hospital, London	Assemblyman; Treasurer, U.S. Mint
Rev. Francis Alison's New London Academy; trained as a surveyor; read law with brother George Smith	Assemblyman; Delegate, Pennsylvania Constitutional Convention
Unknown	Justice of the Peace; Assemblyman; Committee of Correspondence; Indian Commissioner; State Supreme Executive Council
Rev. Francis Alison's New London Academy	Secretary, Continental and Confederation Congresses
University of St. Andrews; read law with John Dickinson	Committee of Correspondence; Assemblyman; Confederation Congressman; Delegate, U.S. Constitutional Convention; Justice, U.S. Supreme Court
Preparatory studies in Bath, England; law studies at Inner Temple, London	Assemblyman; Common Council; City Alderman; Justice, City Court; Justice, Court of Common Pleas; Mayor of Philadelphia; Justice, State Supreme Court; Committees of Correspondence and Safety; President, Bank of North America, Bank of the United States
Harvard	Committees of Safety, Inspection, and Military Defenses; Confederation Congressman; Judge, Chief Justice, Superior Court; Commissioner of Loans; U.S. Collector of Revenue at Newport
Home-schooled	Town Council (President); Assemblyman (Speaker); Justice of the Peace; Judge, Court of Common Pleas; Justice, Chief Justice, Supreme and Superior Courts; Governor
Home-schooled; read law in Charleston, SC; law studies at Middle Temple, London	Provincial Congressman/Assemblyman; Council of Safety; Judge, Court of Common Pleas; Committee to Draft State Constitution
Indigo Society School, Georgetown, SC; Eaton; Cambridge; law studies at Middle Temple, London	Provincial Congressman/Assemblyman
Hackney School; Cambridge University; law studies at Middle Temple, London	Justice of the Peace; Provincial Congressman/Assemblyman; Council of Safety; Confederation Congress
Law studies at Middle Temple, London	Provincial Congressman/Assemblyman; Delegate, South Carolina Constitutional Convention; Governor
William & Mary	Burgess/Assemblyman; County Sheriff; Committee of Safety; Council of State
William & Mary	Burgess/Assemblyman (Speaker); Committee of Correspondence; Governor
William & Mary; read law with George Wythe	Burgess/Assemblyman; Governor; Confederation Minister to France; U.S. Secretary of State; Vice President of the U.S.; President of the U.S.
Private tutoring[?]; Wakefield Academy, Yorkshire, England	Justice of the Peace; Burgess/Assemblyman; Committee of Correspondence; Confederation Congress; President of the United States in Congress Assembled; U.S. Senator
Private tutoring[?]	Burgess/Assemblyman; State Senator
Home-schooled and private school in Gloucester County; Hackney Academy, England; Christ's College, Cambridge	Burgess/Assemblyman; Justice of the Peace; Delegate, Virginia Constitutional Convention; Governor
Home-schooled (by his mother); read law with uncle Stephen Dewey	Burgess/Assemblyman (Clerk, Speaker); Mayor of Williamsburg; Delegate, Virginia Constitutional Convention; Judge, Court of Chancery; Delegate, Virginia Convention to ratify the U.S. Constitution; Chancellor, Courts of Virginia

Robert Morris

Pennsylvania
1735–1806

"Financier of America's Revolution," Robert Morris learned commerce as an apprentice to Philadelphia's Charles Willing and as a partner with his son in a prosperous trading firm. Hurt by the Stamp Act, Morris and Willing sided with the patriots. As a delegate to the Second Continental Congress, Morris raised capital and provisions for the resistance, including by lotteries. Though Morris and John Dickinson had voted against separation, they abstained from a crucial Pennsylvania ballot of 2 July 1776, thereby permitting a colony vote for independence. Morris signed the Declaration in August 1776. His commitment was evident in personal loans and guarantees for army supply. General Washington often relied on Morris and his business connections to supply and transport the Continental Army, including for the final Yorktown campaign. That same year, 1781, Congress made him superintendent of finance to rescue the colonies from a currency collapse. His establishment of a national bank, backed in part by private and foreign credit extensions, stabilized the country's finances at a critical juncture. After the war, Morris argued for stronger central government with separate revenue powers. Once among America's richest, his fortune vanished amid the 1797 panic. Ironically, the "Great Man" who repeatedly buttressed his country's credit with his own ended up in debtors' prison and died in humble circumstances in 1806.

William Paca

Maryland
1740–1799

William Paca, son of a prominent Maryland planter, earned B.A. and M.A. degrees from the College of Philadelphia and was admitted to the Maryland Bar, all before he turned 22. Affluent by birth and more so by marriage, Paca's political career began in 1765 when, with Samuel Chase, he organized the Anne Arundel County Sons of Liberty to oppose the Stamp Act. Elected in 1767 to the Maryland General Assembly, Paca was an articulate strategist for colonist rights, earning appointment in 1774 as a delegate to the First Continental Congress. In 1777, he helped raise militia forces on Maryland's Eastern Shore to resist British and Tory incursions. Yet he also resisted illegal actions by patriot forces, telling one officer that if he "attempted to seize any of my Horses I would blow his Brains out." Paca subsequently served as a judge on Maryland's General Court and the U.S. Court of Appeals, then as Maryland's governor for the maximum of three one-year terms. In 1787, he was elected as an antifederalist delegate to Maryland's convention to consider ratifying the new U.S. Constitution. Although Paca's 22 amendments were defeated, they embodied the first systematic proposal for a bill of rights, influencing other state conventions to press for what became the first 10 amendments to the Constitution.

Caesar Rodney

Delaware
1728–1784

Delaware's best known patriot, Caesar Rodney inherited his father's Dover plantation at 17, giving him the means to support a life of public service. In addition to serving in numerous Kent County offices, including sheriff, justice of the peace, and militia captain, Rodney was elected to the Delaware Assembly in 1758. As a delegate to the Stamp Act Congress, he supported demands for jury trials and colonial approval of taxation. Becoming speaker of the Delaware Assembly in 1769, Rodney helped form the colony's committee of correspondence to organize resistance against Britain's coercive policies and was sent to the Continental Congress with Thomas McKean and George Read. On 1 July 1776, with McKean and Read split on Delaware's vote on independence, McKean summoned Rodney, then in Lewes, Delaware. Rodney traveled 80 miles through nighttime thunderstorms, arriving at the Pennsylvania State House the next morning to break the deadlock and help Congress achieve unanimity. Though loyalist backlash soon voted Rodney out of his legislative roles, he continued to serve in Delaware's militia, rising to become its commanding officer. In March 1778, he was elected state president and did his best to rally resources during three perilous years. He was then re-elected to Congress, but could not serve due to failing health. Rodney had long suffered from a cancer that disfigured his face. He died in 1784, providing for the gradual emancipation of his slaves through his will.

Francis Lewis (1713–1802)

NEW YORK. Prominent merchant and delegate to Congress from 1775 to 1779, Lewis, like other New York delegates, had to abstain from voting for independence in July 1776, but was among the first to sign the Declaration on 2 August. Later that year, British forces pillaged his home and captured his wife, who was freed after George Washington took two Tory women in retaliation and brokered an exchange.

Philip Livingston (1716–1778)

NEW YORK. A Yale-educated merchant and leading New York City philanthropist, Livingston strongly criticized parliamentary taxation and helped finance and supply patriot forces. Yet fearing civil unrest, he was hesitant about independence, characterizing it in 1774 as "the most vain, empty, shallow, and ridiculous project." Absent during the July 1776 votes on independence, he signed the Declaration in August.

Thomas Lynch, Jr. (1749–1779)

SOUTH CAROLINA. A Cambridge-educated lawyer, rice planter, and militia captain, Lynch was sent to Congress in 1776 to join his ailing father, who had suffered a stroke. The younger Lynch voted for and signed the Declaration. He was lost at sea in 1779.

Arthur Middleton (1742–1787)

SOUTH CAROLINA. A London-educated lawyer and one of South Carolina's wealthiest planters, Middleton was among the more radical South Carolina rebels. Elected to Congress in the spring of 1776, his service there was sporadic. As an officer defending Charleston, he was captured and held prisoner for a year.

Lewis Morris (1726–1798)

NEW YORK. Third lord of Morrisania Manor, Morris was a conservative Whig who sought to protect his patrician class while opposing Parliament. Sent to Congress in 1775, he missed the July 1776 vote for independence while leading the Westchester militia and helping Washington defend New York. He signed the Declaration in August. His estate was plundered by both armies; he rebuilt it after the war.

John Morton (1725–1777)

PENNSYLVANIA. Farmer, surveyor, lawyer, and judge from Chester County, Morton, a moderate, was unanimously elected speaker of Pennsylvania's assembly in 1774. With Franklin and Wilson, he turned Pennsylvania's vote for independence on 2 July, an action he characterized as "the most glorious service I ever rendered my county." He was the first signer to die, on 1 April 1777.

Thomas Nelson (1738–1789)

VIRGINIA. A Cambridge-educated planter and merchant from Yorktown, Nelson was among the most radical members of the House of Burgesses. In May 1776, he helped write Virginia's resolutions for independence and delivered them to Congress. He returned to command Virginia's militia. Replacing Thomas Jefferson as governor in 1781, he provided critical support for victory at Yorktown.

Robert Treat Paine (1731–1814)

MASSACHUSETTS. Harvard-trained minister, seaman, and state justice, Paine came to prominence in 1770 for prosecuting those accused in the Boston Massacre, despite losing to defender John Adams. In Congress from 1774 to 1776, he specialized in military supply and was dubbed the "objection maker" for his habit of challenging proposals. He later helped to establish the American Academy of Arts and Sciences.

John Penn (1740–1788)

NORTH CAROLINA. After a decade practicing law in Virginia, Penn moved to Granville County, North Carolina, in 1774. Rising quickly in provincial politics, he was sent to Congress in 1775. He declared early, "My first wish is that America be free." Except for one year, Penn remained active in Congress until 1780, when he was recalled to serve on North Carolina's board of war and governor's council.

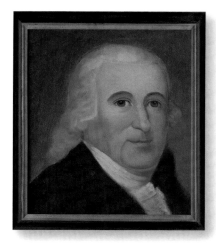

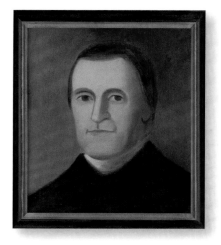

Benjamin Rush

Pennsylvania
1746–1813

Physician, professor, writer, social activist, Benjamin Rush was a "revolutionary gadfly." Fatherless at five, Rush was educated at an uncle's Maryland academy and at the College of New Jersey (Princeton), finishing an A.B. at 14. Following five years of medical apprenticeship in Philadelphia, Rush went to the University of Edinburgh to earn his medical degree. As a physician and professor at the College of Philadelphia, Rush cultivated friendships with Thomas Jefferson, John Adams, and Thomas Paine, urging the last to write *Common Sense*, which played a key role in turning public sentiment toward independence. Rush became a delegate to the Continental Congress in late July 1776, and signed the Declaration of Independence in August. In April 1778, he was appointed as a surgeon-general for the Continental Army, but resigned the following January after criticizing Washington and the administration of the Continental Army. Rush became internationally renowned as a medical educator, though his reliance on bleeding was disparaged, particularly during Philadelphia's yellow fever outbreak in 1793. Rush was also famous for supporting a wide range of public causes, including the abolition of slavery and capital punishment, temperance, prison reform, universal public education, free health care, religion in schools, humane treatment of mental illness, and a "peace office." He also supported the U.S. Constitution and served as treasurer of the U.S. Mint (1797–1813). His last service was helping Adams and Jefferson reconcile their differences in 1812.

Edward Rutledge

South Carolina
1749–1800

Son of a South Carolina physician and planter, Rutledge studied law in London where he observed the workings of Parliament. Shortly after his return, he gained the attention of patriots for successfully defending a jailed colonial publisher. In 1774, Rutledge was sent to the Continental Congress, and, upon the withdrawal of senior delegates, became South Carolina's delegation leader. Delegation hopes for reconciliation with Britain cooled when Virginia's royal governor offered to emancipate slaves who fought for the British. Still, Rutledge resisted motions to declare independence. As late as 8 June 1776, he wrote that no reason existed for the measure "but the reason of every madman." As an alternative, Rutledge advocated forming a substantial confederation of rebelling colonies and securing foreign alliances. Not until 2 July did he commit himself and his delegation to vote for independence, and then only because he saw the need for unity. Rutledge was the youngest to sign the Declaration at age 27. He soon left Congress to serve in South Carolina's legislature and militia. He was captured during the defense of Charleston and held prisoner for nearly a year. After the war, he served as a conservative state legislator until elected governor in 1799. He died in office the next year at age 50.

Roger Sherman

Connecticut
1721–1793

Remembered as a "venerable uncorrupted patriot," Roger Sherman was born and raised in small towns outside Boston where he received limited formal schooling. In 1742, he moved his family to Connecticut, where over time he established himself as a successful surveyor, land speculator, merchant, lawyer, and publisher of a popular annual almanac. His political career began in 1748. After holding several local posts, he was elected to the Connecticut General Assembly in 1754. Esteemed for his integrity, incisive thinking, and plain-spoken opposition to Parliament, Sherman was sent to the Continental Congress in 1774. Persevering in that role until the war's end, he served on the vital committees of war and treasury, as well as the five-man committee tasked to draft the Declaration of Independence. John Adams later characterized Sherman as "one of the soundest and strongest pillars of the Revolution." Until his death in 1793, Sherman continued to serve in both state and national legislatures. His most enduring contributions came at the 1787 Constitutional Convention. He gave more than 130 speeches, defending the interests of smaller states while supporting a strong central government. The best known product of his negotiating efforts is the "Connecticut Compromise," which gave states parity in the U.S. Senate. Among Sherman's many admirers, Thomas Jefferson described him as "a man who never said a foolish thing in his life."

James Wilson

Pennsylvania
1742–1798

A key American constitutional figure, James Wilson was born and educated in Scotland. After abandoning training for ministry, he emigrated to Philadelphia in 1765, where he studied law under John Dickinson. His influential 1774 pamphlet, *Considerations on the Nature and Extent of the Legislative Authority of the British Parliament,* argued that because "all power is derived from the people," Parliament had no authority over the colonies since it denied them representation, and the king deserved allegiance only so long as he protected the people. Thomas Jefferson copied sections in a personal notebook and may have used them in drafting the Declaration. As a Pennsylvania delegate to the Continental Congress, Wilson delayed measures for independence following instructions to the delegation to resist "separation." Once that restriction was lifted in late June 1776, Wilson supported independence. At the 1787 Constitutional Convention, Wilson's influence was second only to Madison's. His proposals, which included direct election of both houses of Congress and the president, were arguably the most "democratic." Scholars have credited his contributions to constitutional debates with forming the basis of Federalist thought. Wilson subsequently taught law and served on the U.S. Supreme Court. Ironically, his critics deemed him anti-democratic for defending Quaker loyalists, opposing price controls, and promoting the creation of a national bank. Overextended borrowing landed Wilson in debtors' prison in 1797, and he died the following year in North Carolina while evading creditors.

John Witherspoon

New Jersey
1723–1794

Educator, churchman, and patriot, John Witherspoon was the only clergyman to sign the Declaration. Born in Scotland, he earned an M.A. and studied divinity at the University of Edinburgh. As a Presbyterian minister active in Scottish church politics, Witherspoon's satirical critiques of arbitrary ecclesiastical power earned him international acclaim and an invitation to become president of the College of New Jersey (later Princeton). Arriving in 1768, he implemented key curricular changes and advocated resistance to British colonial policies through his lectures, sermons, writings, and actions, such as conferring honorary degrees upon John Dickinson and John Hancock. Witherspoon's reputed "seminary of sedition" attracted and trained emerging patriot leaders from across the colonies, including James Madison. In 1774, he wrote that colonists "prefer war with all its horrors, and even extermination itself to slavery." Sent to Congress as a New Jersey delegate in June 1776, Witherspoon is said to have argued on 2 July that the colonies were "not only ripe" for independence "but in danger of rotting for the want of it." He remained active in Congress throughout the Revolution, serving on key committees on war and secret correspondence. His oldest son was killed at Germantown. After the war, he remained politically engaged as a legislator and advocate for the new Constitution. He also worked to rebuild the College of New Jersey and unify the Presbyterian Church in America.

George Read (1733–1798)

DELAWARE. Distinguished New Castle lawyer and patriot, Read joined with Pennsylvania's John Dickinson in voting against independence on 2 July 1776, deeming it premature. Read, however, signed the Declaration in August. His calming leadership reintegrated loyalist and neutral figures into Delaware politics. Pleased by compromises reached in drafting the federal Constitution, he led Delaware to be the first state to ratify it in 1787.

George Ross (1730–1779)

PENNSYLVANIA. Former royal prosecutor for Cumberland County, Ross represented Lancaster from 1768 to 1775 in the provincial assembly, where he increasingly criticized British policies. Pennsylvania's Constitutional Convention sent him to Congress on 20 July 1776, and he signed the Declaration on 2 August. Ross later helped draft Pennsylvania's Declaration of Rights, and worked to moderate its radical first constitution.

James Smith (1719–1806)

PENNSYLVANIA. Irish immigrant, surveyor, lawyer, and ardent Whig, Smith in 1774 proposed a boycott on British goods and organized a volunteer militia company. At a June 1776 provincial convention, he helped draft resolutions urging independence. On 20 July, he was sent to Congress and signed the Declaration. Congress used his York law offices during 1778 after having to evacuate Philadelphia.

Richard Stockton (1730–1781)

NEW JERSEY. A successful lawyer, Stockton spent 1766-67 in London, where he met the king and recruited John Witherspoon to head the College of New Jersey. Upon his return, he was appointed royal councilor and later supreme court justice. Arriving in Congress on 1 July 1776, he voted for independence the next day. He was captured by British authorities in November and imprisoned for four months.

Thomas Stone (1743–1787)

MARYLAND. A large landowner and successful lawyer, Stone was sent to Congress in 1775. A more conservative revolutionary than fellow Maryland delegates William Paca and Samuel Chase, he endorsed using poll tax revenues to support the Episcopal church and favored reconciliation up to July 1776. A month after signing the Declaration, he advocated peace negotiations with British general Lord Howe.

George Taylor (1716–1781)

PENNSYLVANIA. Raised in northern Ireland, Taylor settled in Pennsylvania, where he was ironmaster, militia captain, magistrate, and North Hampton delegate to the provincial assembly. Pennsylvania's Constitutional Convention sent him to Congress on 20 July 1776. He signed the Declaration on 2 August. His Durham forge produced ammunition for the Revolution, but his business partner turned Tory in late 1776.

Matthew Thornton (1714?–1803)

NEW HAMPSHIRE. Born in Ireland, Thornton's family emigrated to Massachusetts when he was three. A practicing physician, he later became a leader in the colony's provincial congress. In December 1775, he chaired the committee that wrote a state constitution, the first of its kind. Not appointed to Congress until September 1776, he signed the Declaration on 4 November.

George Walton (1749?–1804)

GEORGIA. Raised near Farmville, Virginia, at 20 Walton moved to Savannah, where he studied law and helped to organize Georgia's late-blooming patriot efforts. He arrived in Congress on 1 July 1776, in time to vote for independence. Commissioned in Georgia's militia, he was captured in 1778 and held prisoner. Following his release, he served as state legislator, judge, and governor.

William Whipple (1730–1785)

NEW HAMPSHIRE. A ship captain by age 21, Whipple's cargoes included wood, rum, and slaves. With his fortune secured as a Portsmouth merchant, he became an ardent patriot and a delegate to Congress, serving from early 1776 through 1779. Appointed state militia general in 1777, Whipple's unit escorted Burgoyne's surrendered army from Albany to Boston.

William Williams (1731–1811)

CONNECTICUT. A Harvard-educated merchant, Williams served for over 50 years in local, colonial, and state offices. A central figure in Connecticut's revolutionary politics, he served as committee of correspondence clerk, assembly speaker, and organizer of the council of safety. His service in Congress began on 28 July 1776. He signed the Declaration on 2 August.

Oliver Wolcott (1726–1797)

CONNECTICUT. A Yale graduate whose career included medicine, commerce, and law, Wolcott was appointed to several terms in Congress between October 1775 and April 1783. Frequently absent while commanding Connecticut's militia, in July 1776 he famously had an equestrian statue of King George III melted into bullets (see p. 10). Illness kept him away when the Declaration was adopted, though he signed it during the fall of 1776.

George Wythe (1726?–1806)

VIRGINIA. "Father of American jurisprudence," Wythe was an ardent "independence man" in Congress. He missed the July 1776 votes on independence while working on Virginia's constitution, but signed the Declaration in late August. As governor in 1779, Thomas Jefferson appointed his mentor America's first law professor at the College of William and Mary. Wythe also served for a quarter century as an appellate judge.

Names	Residence	Copies	Parchment
Th. Jefferson	Monticello	1 copy	parchment
James Madison	Montpellier	1	D° or paid
J. Q. Adams paid also p 7/N	Washington	1	1 pd
Wm H. Crawford	do Washington	1 paid	1 paid
J. C. Calhoun	do Washington	1	1 paid
B W Crowninshield	Washington	1	1 paid
H. Clay	Lexington (K)	1	1
Eldred Simkins	Edgefield C. House N.C.	1	1
Jas. Owen	Bladen County ct. of Ga		1
Daniel D Tompkins	Castleton, Staten Is. (N.Y.)	1	1 paid
Alex Richard	Madrid St. Lawrence N.Y.		

Document Gallery

The PENNSYLVANIA EVENING POST.

Price only Two Coppers.   Publifhed every *Tuefday*, *Thurfday*, and *Saturday* Evenings.

Vol. II.]   SATURDAY, JULY 6, 1776.   [Num. 228.

In CONGRESS, July 4, 1776.
A Declaration by the Reprefentatives of the United States of America, in General Congrefs affembled.

WHEN, in the courfe of human events, it becomes neceffary for one people to diffolve the political bands which have connected them with another, and to affume, among the powers of the earth, the feparate and equal ftation to which the laws of nature and of nature's God intitle them, a decent refpect to the opinions of mankind requires that they fhould declare the caufes which impel them to the feparation.

We hold thefe truths to be felf-evident, That all men are created equal ; that they are endowed, by their Creator, with certain unalienable rights ; that among thefe are life, liberty, and the purfuit of happinefs. That to fecure thefe rights, governments are inftituted among men, deriving their juft powers from the confent of the governed ; that whenever any form of government becomes deftructive of thefe ends, it is the right of the people to alter or to abolifh it, and to inftitute new government, laying its foundation on fuch principles, and organizing its powers in fuch form, as to them fhall feem moft likely to effect their fafety and happinefs. Prudence, indeed, will dictate that governments long eftablifhed fhould not be changed for light and tranfient caufes ; and accordingly all experience hath fhewn, that mankind are more difpofed to fuffer, while evils are fufferable, than to right themfelves by abolifhing the forms to which they are accuftomed. But when a long train of abufes and ufurpations, purfuing invariably the fame object, evinces a defign to reduce them under abfolute defpotifm, it is their right, it is their duty, to throw off fuch government, and to provide new guards for their future fecurity. Such has been the patient fufferance of thefe colonies, and fuch is now the neceffity which conftrains them to alter their former fyftems of government. The hiftory of the prefent King of Great-Britain is a hiftory of repeated injuries and ufurpations, all having in direct object the eftablifhment of an abfolute tyranny over thefe ftates. To prove this, let facts be fubmitted to a candid world.

He has refufed his affent to laws, the moft wholefome and neceffary for the public good.

He has forbidden his Governors to pafs laws of immediate and preffing importance, unlefs fufpended in their operation till his affent fhould be obtained ; and, when fo fufpended, he has utterly neglected to attend to them.

He has refufed to pafs other laws for the accommodation of large diftricts of people, unlefs thofe people would relinquifh the right of reprefentation in the legiflature, a right ineftimable to them, and formidable to tyrants only.

He has called together legiflative bodies at places unufual, uncomfortable, and diftant from the depofitory of their public records, for the fole purpofe of fatiguing them into compliance with his meafures.

He has diffolved Reprefentative Houfes repeatedly, for oppofing with manly firmnefs his invafions on the rights of the people.

He has refufed for a long time, after fuch diffolutions, to caufe others to be elected ; whereby the legiflative powers, incapable of annihilation, have returned to the people at large for their exercife ; the ftate remaining in the mean time expofed to all the dangers of invafion from without, and convulfions within.

He has endeavoured to prevent the population of thefe ftates ; for that purpofe obftructing the laws for naturalization of foreigners ; refufing to pafs others to encourage their migrations hither, and raifing the conditions of new appropriations of lands.

He has obftructed the adminiftration of juftice, by refufing his affent to laws for eftablifhing judiciary powers.

He has made Judges dependant on his will alone, for the tenure of their offices, and the amount and payment of their falaries.

He has erected a multitude of new offices, and fent hither fwarms of officers to harrafs our people, and eat out their fubftance.

He has kept among us, in times of peace, ftanding armies, without the confent of our legiflatures.

He has affected to render the military independant of and fuperior to the civil power.

He has combined with others to fubject us to a jurifdiction foreign to our conftitution, and unacknowledged by our laws ; giving his affent to their acts of pretended legiflation :

For quartering large bodies of armed troops among us :

For protecting them, by a mock trial, from punifhment for any murders which they fhould commit on the inhabitants of thefe ftates :

For cutting off our trade with all parts of the world :

For impofing taxes on us without our confent :

For depriving us, in many cafes, of the benefits of trial by jury :

For tranfporting us beyond feas to be tried for pretended offences :

For abolifhing the free fyftem of Englifh laws in a neighbouring province, eftablifhing therein an arbitrary government, and enlarging its boundaries, fo as to render it at once an example and fit inftrument for introducing the fame abfolute rule into thefe colonies :

For taking away our charters, abolifhing our moft valuable laws, and altering fundamentally the forms of our governments :

For fufpending our own legiflatures, and declaring themfelves invefted with power to legiflate for us in all cafes whatfoever.

He has abdicated government here, by declaring us out of his protection and waging war againft us.

He has plundered our feas, ravaged our coafts, burnt our towns, and deftroyed the lives of our people.

He is, at this time, tranfporting large armies of foreign mercenaries to complete the works of death, defolation, and tyranny, already begun with circumftances of cruelty and

---

***Pennyslvania Evening Post*, 6 July 1776.**

Not surprisingly, the first newspaper printing of the Declaration appeared in Philadelphia, where Congress had voted for independence. Benjamin Towne published the complete text on the front page of his *Pennsylvania Evening Post* on 6 July 1776. At the time, Towne professed himself a patriot to gain advantage over rivals, but when British forces occupied Philadelphia beginning in fall 1777, he switched loyalties to remain in operation. Later, John Witherspoon helped Towne craft a recantation that was published widely, enabling him to stay in business despite a tarnished reputation.

NEW YORK, July 1.

IN consequence of an information lately made, that sundry persons had entered into a solemn agreement to aid and assist our unnatural enemies in making themselves masters of our city, several of them were apprehended; and on Friday last one of those conspirators, a soldier in his excellency general Washington's guards, was executed in a field near this city, in the presence of a multitude of spectators.

We hear that four more transports with troops, besides those already mentioned, have been taken, and carried into some of our ports to the eastward.

On Sunday last one of our cruisers, on the south side of Long Island, took a large Bermudian built sloop from Halifax, laden with intrenching tools, &c. bound for this place; in which a number of the Boston refugees are on board, among whom, it is said, is Robert Auchmuty, esq; late judge of the admiralty at Boston, and brother to the rev. doctor Auchmuty, of this city.

It is currently reported, that our cruisers have taken 13 sail of transports to the eastward.

July 4. Last Saturday arrived at the Hook (like a swarm of locusts escaped from the bottomless pit) a fleet said to be 130 sail of ships and vessels from Halifax, having on board general Howe, &c. sent out by the tyrants of Great Britain, after destroying the English constitution there, on the pious design of enslaving the British colonies, and plundering their property at pleasure, or murdering them at once, and taking possession of all, as Ahab did of Naboth's vineyard.

On Monday about 1000 of them landed on the west end of Long Island, but soon embarked again; and seeing a party of riflemen, said to be about 1000, gave them three huzzas, which they returned with the Indian war whoop. On Tuesday morning some of them appeared coming up, and before night about 45 sail came above the Narrows and anchored at and near the Watering Place, where they fired about 50 cannon shot, of which we have not heard the occasion, and landed many of their men, whom we could plainly see exercising and parading.

It was apprehended they intended to penetrate into the interior parts of the island, or to some of the neighbouring towns; but it does not appear that they have yet attempted it, or done any thing on shore, except taking up a little bridge on the causeway between the landing and the highlands, at the ferry. We hear general Mercer, with a detachment, was yesterday despatched to watch their motions, and act as occasion might require.

We are assured that major Lamb, capt. Oswald, and capt. Burr, are prisoners on board this fleet.

PHILADELPHIA, July 4.

A LETTER from the camp at Sorel, dated June 13th, gives a more favourable account of the loss we sustained in the attack of the enemy at Three Rivers, and concludes as follows: " Our loss is inconsiderable as to numbers, but, alas! not so as to men, general Thompson being among the prisoners. Though we had the worst of it, I hope we have made some impression on the minds of our enemies. They allow us behaved well; and it will not tell amiss that 1200 Americans attacked, under every disadvantage, 4000 British troops, obliged them at first to give way, and, when beat back, made a retreat of 45 miles with the loss of about 150 men."

By accounts from Canada, we learn that our army have retreated to Isle aux Noix, from whence they have sent their sick and baggage to Crown Point.

July 8. This day, at 12 o'clock, the declaration of INDEPENDENCE will be proclaimed at the Statehouse.

Abstract from the minutes of the General Congress, of Thursday the 4th instant, declaring the United Colonies free and independent states, which will be published at full length in next week's Gazette. The first part of the declaration is a recapitulation of injuries, and it concludes as follows:

IN every stage of these oppressions, we have petitioned for redress in the most humble terms. Our repeated petitions have been answered only by repeated injury. A prince whose character is thus marked, by every act which may define a TYRANT, is unfit to be the ruler of a FREE PEOPLE.

Nor have we been wanting in attentions to our British brethren. We have warned them, from time to time, of attempts by their legislature to extend an unwarrantable jurisdiction over us. We have reminded them of the circumstances of our emigration and settlement here. We have appealed to their native justice and magnanimity, and we have conjured them by the ties of our common kindred to disavow these usurpations, which would inevitably interrupt our connexions and correspondence. They too have been deaf to the voice of justice and consanguinity. We must therefore acquiesce in the necessity which denounces our separation, and hold them (as we hold the rest of mankind) enemies in war; in peace, friends.

We therefore, the representatives of the UNITED STATES OF AMERICA, in GENERAL CONGRESS assembled, appealing to the Supreme Judge of the world for the rectitude of our intentions, do, in the name and by the authority of the good people of these colonies, solemnly publish and declare, that these United Colonies are, and of right ought to be, FREE AND INDEPENDENT STATES; that they are absolved from all allegiance to the British crown, and that all political connexion between them and the state of Great Britain is, and ought to be, totally dissolved; and that, as FREE and INDEPENDENT STATES, they have full power to levy war, conclude peace, contract alliances, establish commerce, and to do all other acts and things which INDEPENDENT STATES may of right do. And for the support of this declaration, with a firm reliance on the protection of Divine Providence, we mutually pledge to each other our lives, our fortunes, and our sacred honour.

Signed by order and in behalf of the Congress,
JOHN HANCOCK, president.

WAR OFFICE, Philadelphia, July 6, 1776.

ALL persons in the United American States who are able to inform the Congress of any quantities of flint stone, or of any persons who are skilled in the manufacture of FLINTS, are requested to apply in person, or by letter, to the Board of War and Ordnance, at the War Office, in Market street, near the corner of Fourth street.---- All printers of newspapers in the several States are desired to insert this advertisement.

RICHARD PETERS, jun. secretary.

ANNAPOLIS, July 11.

YESTERDAY evening six companies of the first battalion of Maryland troops stationed in this city, commanded by col. William Smallwood, embarked for the head of Elk in high spirits; and three companies of the same battalion, stationed in Baltimore town, embarked yesterday morning for the same place, from whence they are to proceed to Philadelphia.

Extract of a letter from Philadelphia, dated July 6, 1776, Saturday morning.

" General Howe has landed a great body of troops on Staten island; his force cannot be ascertained. General Washington and his troops are in high spirits. The strength of our army at New York cannot be ascertain-

tained; the militia pour in so fast that it is impracticable. The Jersey militia, amounting to 3500, have acquired great honour in forming and marching with such alacrity and expedition. They have for some time past got over to New York. The battalions of this city (every one of them) are marching to Trenton and Brunswick, in the Jerseys. The rifle battalion, in the pay of this province, marched yesterday for the same places. The militia in the counties are also ordered to march. Out of these bodies they mean to form their quota of the flying camp, to be posted in the Jerseys, and to be at the command of general Washington. It is expected that the Lower Counties and Maryland will immediately march their quotas of militia, to compose the flying camp to this city, to defend it in the absence of its own battalions.

" Your hour of trial is come; your plighted faith, your publick honour, the love of your country, and its dearest liberties, in this moment of imminent danger, demand that you instantly fly to the assistance of a sister colony.

Saturday noon.

" An express is just arrived from general Washington. Howe's army consists of 10 000 men. Admiral Howe is not yet arrived, but hourly expected with 150 sail, having on board 20,000 troops. The enemy's grand army will consist of 30,000. The whole militia of this province are ordered to the Jerseys. We are in anxious expectation to hear from Maryland, nor can we for a moment entertain a doubt that our brethren will desert us in the day of our distress. The farmers here have left their harvest, and cast away the scythe for the musket. I should rejoice to hear you have imitated so laudable, so glorious an example."

WILLIAMSBURG, July 19.

FROM Hampton we learn, that advice was brought there from the Eastern Shore of a tender, mounting two carriage and twelve swivel guns, being drove ashore in a squall of wind, five or six days ago, with 18 pirates on board, among them mr. JAMES PARKER, late of Norfolk, merchant; who immediately surrendered themselves to a party of our troops, and begged for quarters. A boat from another tender, her consort, attempted to cut her out from the creek where she was secured; but our people, perceiving their design, lay in ambush for them, and, when nigh enough, rushed into the water and fired upon them, killing five of the crew, it was supposed, as three were seen to fall overboard, and two to drop down in the boat, upon which the pirates tacked about, and rowed, faster than they came, to their tender.

Benjamin Woodward, against whom an information was lodged for attempting to counterfeit the paper currency of the American states, was brought to town last Wednesday, with four other persons, suspected to be accomplices, and lodged in the publick jail. They were taken in Pittsylvania county, with types and other implements to carry on their wicked and destructive schemes.

Of the vast number of shells which were thrown against Fort Sullivan, near Charlestown, but two fell into it, and only one of them did any execution. The express that brought general Lee's letter, and who may be depended upon, assures us, that the following is an exact list of the loss we sustained by that shell, viz. three ducks, one goose, and a turkey, killed; and one goose so wounded that the cock despaired of its life, and therefore cut off its head.

Lord Dunmore's pestilential fleet was seen last Sunday morning at the mouth of Potowmack.

The following is a particular account of the attack and rout of lord Dunmore, with his piratical crew, from Gwyn's island.

WE got to the island on Monday the 8th, and next morning, at 8 o'clock, began a furious attack upon the enemy's

---

Alexander Purdie's *Virginia Gazette*, 19 July 1776.

Printing was a competitive business in early America, a fact that helped speed the dissemination of news about the Declaration notwithstanding the slow pace of travel and communications in the pre-industrial era. Alexander Purdie operated one of three newspapers in Williamsburg, Virginia, that bore the name *Virginia Gazette*. Purdie published a notice and selected paragraphs from the Declaration on page two of his 19 July 1776 issue, beating his rivals by a day. He published the complete text the following Friday.

Newport, Rhode Island, printing of the Declaration, 13 July 1776.

In accordance with congressional orders to publish and distribute copies of the Declaration as widely as possible, newpaper editors printed the text as supplements to their regular issues or as separate single-sheet broadsides. Solomon Southwick, publisher of Rhode Island's *Newport Mercury*, printed this broadside on 13 July 1776 (note the misdated imprint, which reads "June" in this first state).

IN CONGRESS,
JULY 4, 1776.

A DECLARATION
BY THE
REPRESENTATIVES
OF THE
UNITED STATES OF AMERICA,
IN GENERAL CONGRESS ASSEMBLED.

WHEN in the Course of human Events, it becomes neceffary for one People to diffolve the political Bands which have connected them with another, and to affume among the Powers of the Earth, the feparate and equal Station to which the Laws of Nature and of Nature's God entitle them, a decent Refpect to the Opinions of Mankind requires that they fhould declare the Caufes which impel them to the Separation.

We hold thefe Truths to be felf-evident, that all Men are created equal, that they are endowed by their Creator with certain unalienable Rights, that among thefe are Life, Liberty, and the Purfuit of Happinefs:—That to fecure thefe Rights, Governments are inftituted among Men, deriving their juft Powers from the Confent of the Governed, that whenever any Form of Government becomes deftructive of thefe Ends, it is the Right of the People to alter or to abolifh it, and to inftitute new Government, laying its Foundation on fuch Principles, and organizing its Powers in fuch Form, as to them fhall feem moft likely to effect their Safety and Happinefs. Prudence, indeed, will dictate that Governments long eftablifhed fhould not be changed for light and tranfient Caufes; and accordingly all Experience hath fhewn, that Mankind are more difpofed to fuffer, while Evils are fufferable, than to right themfelves by abolifhing the Forms to which they are accuftomed. But when a long Train of Abufes and Ufurpations, purfuing invariably the fame Object, evinces a Defign to reduce them under abfolute Defpotifm, it is their Right, it is their Duty, to throw off fuch Government, and to provide new Guards for their future Security. Such has been the patient Sufferance of thefe Colonies; and fuch is now the Neceffity which conftrains them to alter their former Syftems of Government. The Hiftory of the prefent King of Great-Britain is a Hiftory of repeated Injuries and Ufurpations, all having in direct Object the Eftablifhment of an abfolute Tyranny over thefe States. To prove this, let Facts be fubmitted to a candid World.

He has refufed his Affent to Laws, the moft wholefome and neceffary for the public Good.

He has forbidden his Governors to pafs Laws of immediate and preffing Importance, unlefs fufpended in their Operation until his Affent fhould be obtained; and when fo fufpended, he has utterly neglected to attend to them.

He has refufed to pafs other Laws for the Accommodation of large Diftricts of People, unlefs thofe People would relinquifh the Right of Reprefentation in the Legiflature, a Right ineftimable to them, and formidable to Tyrants only.

He has called together Legiflative Bodies at Places unufual, uncomfortable, and diftant from the Depofitory of their public Records, for the fole Purpofe of fatiguing them into Compliance with his Meafures.

He has diffolved Reprefentative Houfes repeatedly, for oppofing with manly Firmness his Invafions on the Rights of the People.

He has refufed for a long Time, after fuch Diffolutions, to caufe others to be elected; whereby the Legiflative Powers, incapable of Annihilation, have returned to the People at large for their Exercife; the State remaining in the mean Time expofed to all the Dangers of Invafion from without, and Convulfions within.

He has endeavoured to prevent the Population of thefe States; for that Purpofe obftructing the Laws for Naturalization of Foreigners; refufing to pafs others to encourage their Migrations hither, and raifing the Conditions of new Appropriations of Lands.

He has obftructed the Adminiftration of Juftice, by refufing his Affent to Laws for eftablifhing Judiciary Powers.

He has made Judges dependent on his Will alone, for the Tenure of their Offices, and the Amount and Payment of their Salaries.

He has erected a multitude of new Offices, and fent hither Swarms of Officers to harrafs our People, and eat out their Subftance.

He has kept among us, in Times of Peace, Standing Armies, without the Confent of our Legiflatures.

He has affected to render the Military independent of, and fuperior to the Civil Power.

He has combined with others to fubject us to a Jurifdiction foreign to our Conftitution, and unacknowledged by our Laws; giving his Affent to their Acts of pretended Legiflation:

For quartering large Bodies of armed Troops among us:

For protecting them, by a mock Trial, from Punifhment for any Murders which they fhould commit on the Inhabitants of thefe States:

For cutting off our Trade with all Parts of the World:

For impofing Taxes on us without our Confent:

For depriving us, in many Cafes, of the Benefits of Trial by Jury:

For tranfporting us beyond Seas to be tried for pretended Offences:

For abolifhing the free Syftem of Englifh Laws in a neighbouring Province, eftablifhing therein an arbitrary Government, and enlarging its Boundaries, fo as to render it at once an Example and fit Inftrument for introducing the fame abfolute Rule into thefe Colonies.

For taking away our Charters, abolifhing our moft valuable Laws, and altering fundamentally the Forms of our Governments:

For fufpending our own Legiflatures, and declaring themfelves invefted with Power to legiflate for us in all Cafes whatfoever.

He has abdicated Government here, by declaring us out of his Protection and waging War againft us.

He has plundered our Seas, ravaged our Coafts, burnt our Towns, and deftroyed the Lives of our People.

He is, at this Time, tranfporting large Armies of foreign Mercenaries to compleat the Works of Death, Defolation, and Tyranny, already begun with Circumftances of Cruelty and Perfidy fcarcely paralleled in the moft barbarous Ages, and totally unworthy the Head of a civilized Nation.

He has conftrained our Fellow Citizens, taken Captive on the high Seas, to bear Arms againft their Country; to become the Executioners of their Friends and Brethren, or to fall themfelves by their Hands.

He has excited Domeftic Infurrections amongft us, and has endeavoured to bring on the Inhabitants of our Frontiers, the mercilefs Indian Savages, whofe known Rule of Warfare, is an undiftinguifhed Deftruction of all Ages, Sexes, and Conditions.

In every Stage of thefe Oppreffions we have petitioned for Redrefs, in the moft humble Terms: Our repeated Petitions have been anfwered only by repeated Injury.—A Prince, whofe Character is thus marked by every Act which may define a Tyrant, is unfit to be the Ruler of a FREE PEOPLE!

Nor have we been wanting in Attention to our British Brethren. We have warned them from Time to Time of Attempts by their Legiflature to extend an unwarrantable Jurifdiction over us. We have reminded them of the Circumftances of our Emigration and Settlement here. We have appealed to their native Juftice and Magnanimity, and we have conjured them by the Ties of our common Kindred to difavow thefe Ufurpations, which would inevitably interrupt our Connexions and Correfpondence. They too have been deaf to the Voice of Juftice and of Confanguinity. We muft, therefore, acquiefce in the Neceffity which denounces our Separation, and hold them, as we hold the reft of Mankind, Enemies in War; in Peace, Friends.

We, therefore, the Reprefentatives of the UNITED STATES OF AMERICA, in General Congress affembled, appealing to the SUPREME JUDGE of the World for the Rectitude of our Intentions, do, in the Name and by the Authority of the good People of thefe Colonies, folemnly Publifh and Declare, That thefe United Colonies are, and of Right ought to be, Free and Independent States; that they are abfolved from all Allegiance to the British Crown; and that all political Connexion between them and the State of Great-Britain, is, and ought to be totally diffolved; and that as Free and Independent States, they have full Power to levy War, conclude Peace, contract Alliances, eftablifh Commerce, and to do all other Acts and Things which Independent States may of Right do. And for the Support of this Declaration, with a firm Reliance on the Protection of Divine Providence, we mutually pledge to each other our LIVES, our Fortunes, and our SACRED HONOR.

Signed by Order *and in* Behalf *of the* Congress,

JOHN HANCOCK, PRESIDENT.

Attest, CHARLES THOMPSON, Secretary.

In COUNCIL, July 17th, 1776.

ORDERED, That the Declaration of Independence be printed; and a Copy fent to the Minifters of each Parifh, of every Denomination, within this State; and that they feverally be required to read the fame to their refpective Congregations, as foon as divine Service is ended, in the Afternoon, on the firft Lord's-Day after they fhall have received it:—And after fuch Publication thereof, to deliver the faid Declaration to the Clerks of their feveral Towns, or Diftricts; who are hereby required to record the fame in their refpective Town, or Diftrict Books, there to remain as a perpetual Memorial thereof.

In the Name, and by Order of the Council,

R. DERBY, Jun. Prefident.

A true Copy Atteft, JOHN AVERY, Dep. Sec'y.

SALEM, Massachusetts-Bay: Printed by E. Russell, by Order of Authority.

Salem, Massachusetts, printing of the Declaration, 17 July 1776.

On 17 July 1776, Salem printer E. Russell published this single-sheet broadside of the Declaration. The footer includes an ordinance issued by the Massachusetts-Bay council with instructions for its distribution, public reading, and official recording.

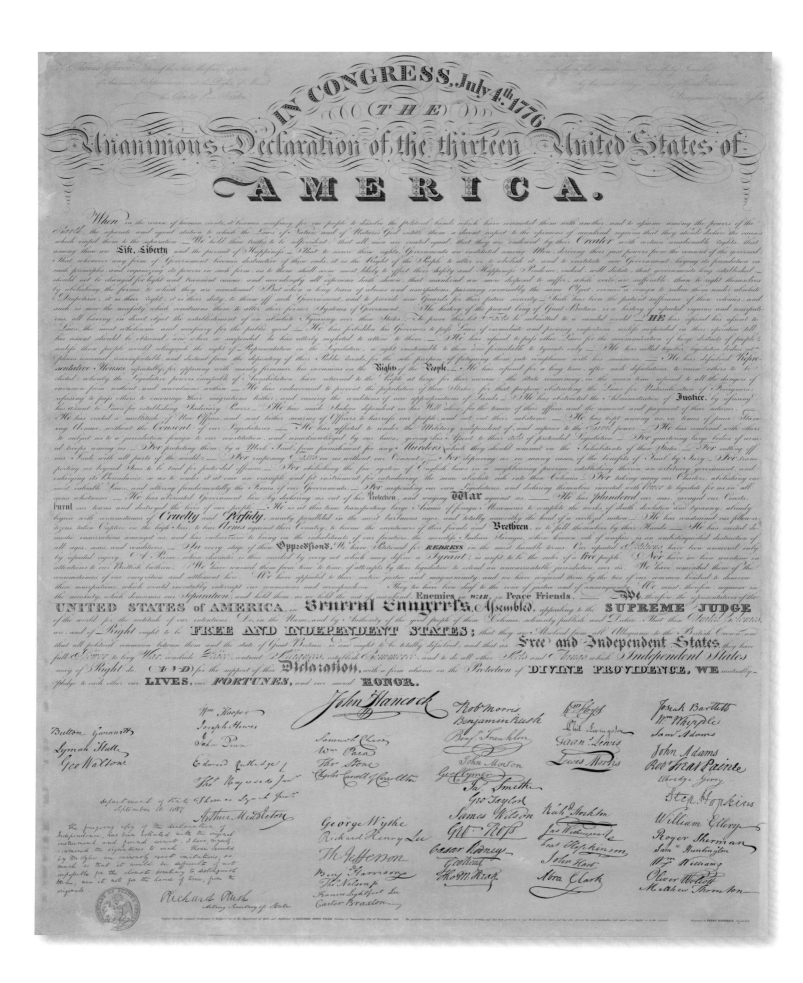

Benjamin Owen Tyler engraving of the Declaration, 1818.

In 1818, Benjamin Owen Tyler published this first commemorative reproduction of the Declaration. The carefully executed engraving, with accurate facsimiles of the signers' autographs, sold well in the patriotic atmosphere that prevailed following American success in the War of 1812.

Benjamin Owen Tyler's subscription book for his engraving of the Declaration, 1815–1818.

Benjamin Tyler recorded subscriptions for his commemorative engraving of the Declaration in this pocket account book. The names of many prominent political figures appear in its pages, beginning with Thomas Jefferson, who acquired a copy printed on parchment.

John Binns's engraving of the Declaration, 1819.

The commercial success of Benjamin Tyler's commemorative engraving of the Declaration prompted other publishers to follow him into a market that was becoming ever more desirous of memorailizing the passing of the signers' generation. This elaborate engraving, issued by John Binns in 1819, is crested with vignettes of George Washington, John Hancock, and Thomas Jefferson, surrounded with medallions representing the thirteen original states.

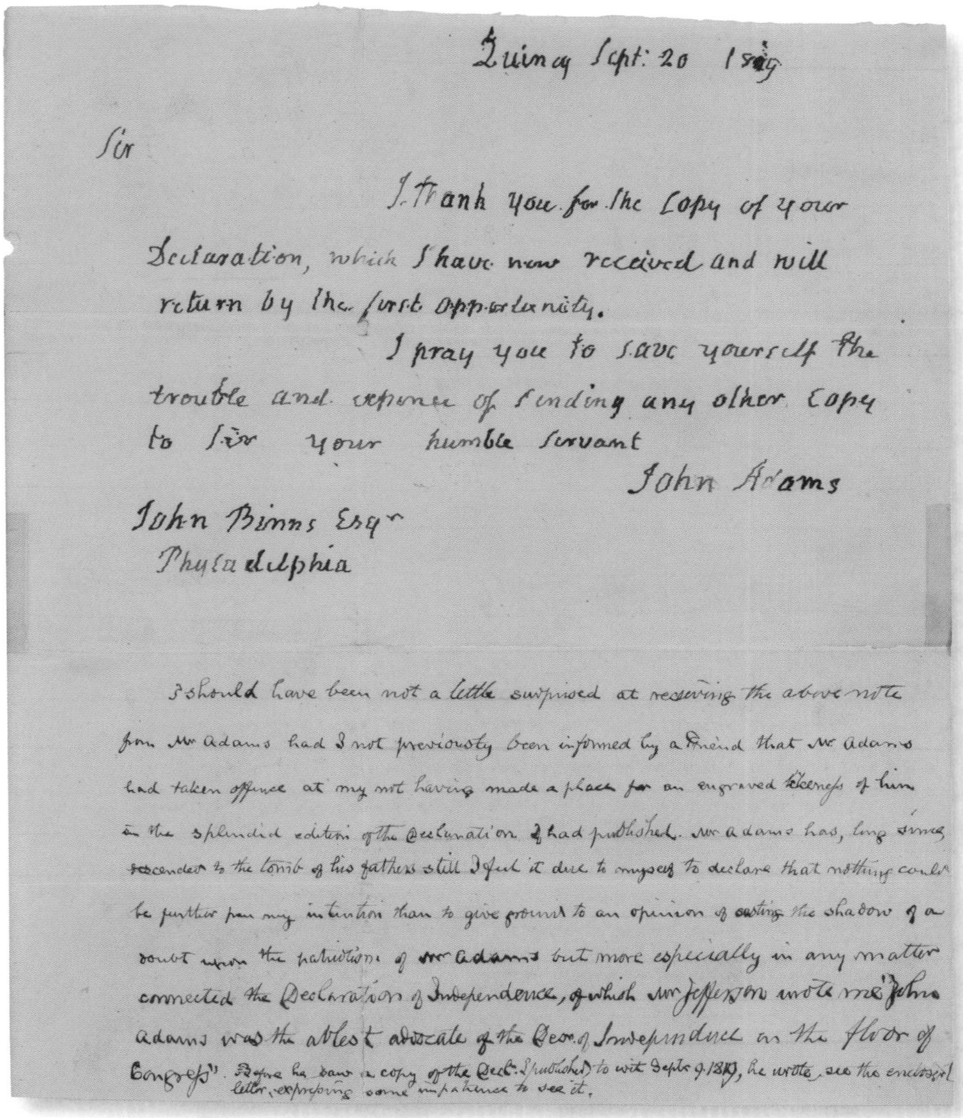

Quincy Sept: 20 1819

Sir

I thank you for the Copy of your Declaration, which I have now received and will return by the first opportunity.

I pray you to save yourself the trouble and expence of sending any other Copy to Sir your humble servant

John Adams

John Binns Esqr
Phyladelphia

I should have been not a little surprised at receiving the above note from Mr Adams had I not previously been informed by a friend that Mr Adams had taken offence at my not having made a place for an engraved likeness of him in the splendid edition of the Declaration I had published. Mr Adams has, long since, descended to the tomb of his fathers still I feel it due to myself to declare that nothing could be further from my intention than to give ground to an opinion of casting the shadow of a doubt upon the patriotism of Mr Adams but more especially in any matter connected the Declaration of Independence, of which Mr Jefferson wrote me "John Adams was the ablest advocate of the Decn of Independence on the floor of Congress". Before he saw a copy of the Decn I published to wit Septr 9 1819, he wrote, see the enclosed letter, expressing some impatience to see it.

Letter of John Adams to John Binns, 20 September 1819.

John Binns sent a copy of his engraving of the Declaration to John Adams, who promptly returned it to him, apparently offended that his image was not featured alongside the other champions of independence and early U.S. presidents. In a shaky hand, the aging Adams, then 84, sent Binns this curt note on 20 September 1819 counseling him to save himself the "trouble and expence [sic] of sending any other copy." Binns penned his reaction in a lengthy note at the bottom of the sheet.

Printing of the Declaration on silk adapted from a design by William Woodruff, after 1820.

In 1819, William Woodruff produced an elaborately decorated engraving of the Declaration similar in concept and style to John Binns's engraving, with its encasing vignettes of George Washington, John Hancock, and Thomas Jefferson and medallions representing the thirteen original states. This printing on silk, an adaptation of Woodruff's design, was produced in Lyon, France, sometime after 1820.

William J. Stone printing of the Declaration, 1823.

In 1823, Secretary of State John Quincy Adams commissioned William J. Stone to produce an official facsimile of the engrossed Declaration on that had been signed by fifty-six delegates from the Second Continental Congress. The original had suffered much wear from repeated travels and showings, and Stone may have left it even more faded by using the common method of moistening its surface to transfer some of the ink to his copper engraving plate. Congress ordered Stone to print two hundred copies of his facsimile on fine vellum for distribution to state legislatures and political leaders. This copy was presented to the Marquis de Lafayette, in gratitude for his service in the Revolutionary War, when he visited the United States in 1824.

Letter of Mercy Otis Warren to Elbridge Gerry, 29 July 1805.

On 29 July 1805, Mercy Otis Warren, the remarkable woman poet and early historian of the Revolution, wrote to signer Elbridge Gerry asking him to confirm Thomas Jefferson's authorship of the Declaration. In his draft response of 20 August, composed on the back of Warren's letter, Gerry reports that when he asked John Adams in 1776 about the document's authorship, Adams replied "Mr. Jefferson drafted it."

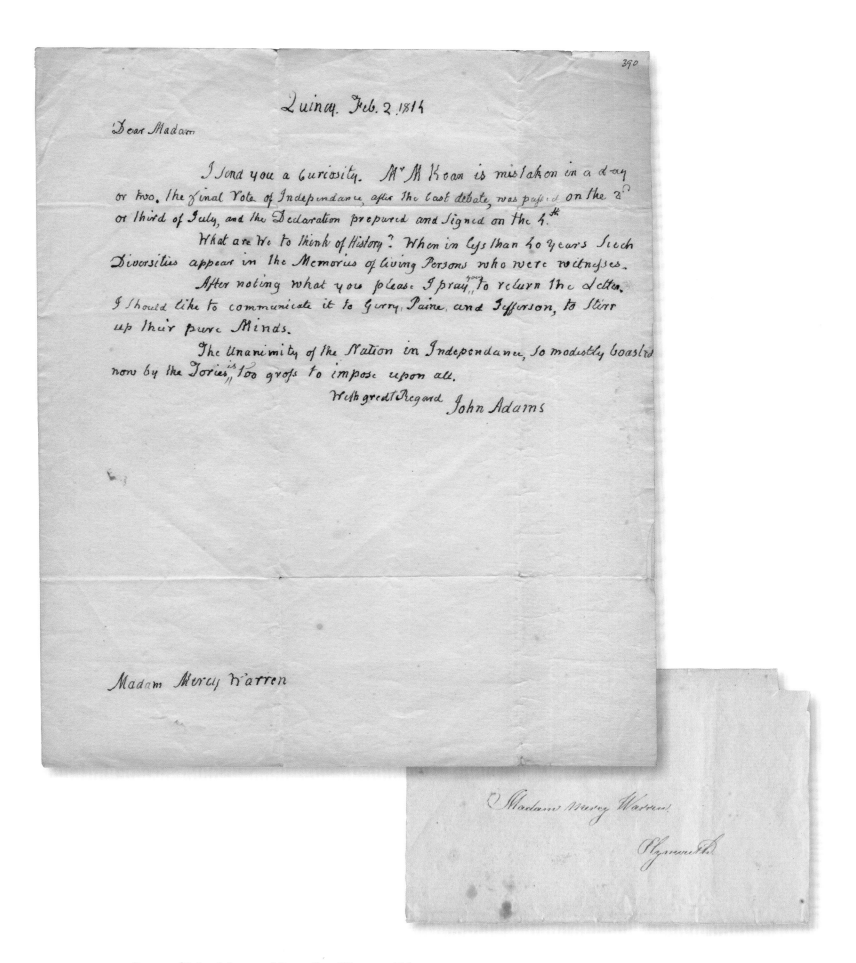

Quincy. Feb. 2. 1814

Dear Madam

I send you a Curiosity. Mr McKean is mistaken in a day or two. The final Vote of Independance, after the last debate, was passed on the 2ᵈ or third of July, and the Declaration prepared and signed on the 4.ᵗʰ

What are We to think of History? When in less than 40 years such Diversities appear in the Memories of living Persons who were witnesses.

After noting what you please. I pray you to return the Letter. I should like to communicate it to Gerry, Paine, and Jefferson, to stirr up their pure Minds.

The Unanimity of the Nation in Independance, so modestly boasted now by the Tories, is too gross to impose upon all.

With great Regard   John Adams

Madam Mercy Warren

Madam Mercy Warren

Plymouth

Letter of John Adams to Mercy Otis Warren, 2 February 1814.

In her three-volume *History of the Rise, Progress, and Termination of the American Revolution* (1805), Mercy Otis Warren charged John Adams with "forgetting the principles of the American revolution." A rift resulted, but the two reconciled in 1812. Together with this letter dated 2 February 1814, Adams forwarded correspondence he had received from Delaware signer Thomas McKean concerning the final vote on independence. Perturbed by the latter's divergent memory of the event, Adams asked Warren to return it to him so that he could send it in turn to fellow signers Elbridge Gerry, Robert Treat Paine, and Thomas Jefferson "to stir up their pure Minds." McKean's letter, acquired separately, is also now part of the Albert H. Small Declaration of Independence Collection.

R. Morris Swander printing of the Declaration, 1865.

This 1865 print by R. Morris Swander features an "allegorical portrait" of George Washington. Washington's image is formed by a cleverly scripted transcription of the Declaration and is surrounded by facsimile signatures of the fifty-six signers, suggesting that the Revolutionary War commander-in-chief and first U.S. president embodied the true spirit and achievement of independence. The broadside is dedicated to the United States Christian Commission, a charitable organization that evangelized and provided welfare service to federal troops during the Civil War.

John Fuller artwork for Declaration lithograph, 1866.

John A. Fuller, a California miner and former East India Company agent, created this decorative pen and ink presentation of the Declaration, titled "Freedom's Footsteps," in 1866. Commemorating the ninetieth anniversary of independence and the end of the Civil War, the design features the text of the Declaration surrounded by the names of the sixteen presidents of the United States and the thirty-six states listed in the order they ratified the Constitution or were admitted to the Union. An elaborate border featuring the names of key revolutionary battles and various patriotic symbols frames the whole. Fuller subsequently had his drawing interpreted into a lithograph and printed in San Francisco. The Albert H. Small Declaration of Independence Collection includes a copy of the lithograph, as well as this original artwork.

71

We hold these Truths to be self-evident

Albert H. Small on the library's central staircase.

RIGHT: *The Albert and Shirley Small Special Collections Library includes a permanent exhibition gallery where highlights from the Albert H. Small Declaration of Independence Collection are kept on public display.*

THE ALBERT H. SMALL DECLARATION OF INDEPENDENCE COLLECTION

Christian Y. Dupont

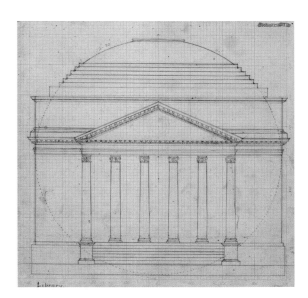

THOMAS JEFFERSON BUILT THE UNIVERSITY OF VIRGINIA around a library, so it is only fitting to have our founder's legacy commemorated by a library collection built around his most singular and consequential achievement—and the one for which he wanted most to be remembered—the Declaration of Independence.

University alumnus Albert Harrison Small ('46) has given his alma mater and the public at large the most comprehensive collection of its kind on the Declaration, and with it, a state-of-the-art library facility that features a permanent exhibition on America's founding document. Each year, thousands of visitors to the Albert and Shirley Small Special Collections Library rediscover and deepen their knowledge of the Declaration, the brave march toward American independence, the struggles of the men and women who fought for it, and the freedoms they won for us all.

Instead of a chapel, Jefferson placed a library at the center of his plans for the University of Virginia. Modeled on the Roman Pantheon, the Rotunda has become the icon of Jefferson's vision for what he described in an 1818 letter as "a system of general instruction, which shall reach every description of our citizens from the richest to the poorest," adding that "as it was the earliest, so will it be the latest of all the public concerns in which I shall permit myself to take an interest."

A third generation Washingtonian, Albert H. Small attended Woodrow Wilson High School before enrolling at the University of Virginia through the V-12 Navy College Training Program. He graduated from the School of Engineering and Applied Science with a chemical engineering degree in 1946, then fulfilled his navy service. He later attended law school at George Washington University and the graduate business school at American University.

During the postwar years, Small began developing affordable homes for veterans in the Maryland suburbs of Washington, D.C. His success soon led to more ambitious projects and the founding of the Southern Engineering Corporation in 1950. Under his leadership, Southern Engineering has built thousands of single-family homes, more than 10,000 apartment units, and several million square feet of new office space in the greater Washington area, in addition to residential and commercial projects in Baltimore, Norfolk, and Richmond. In 2006, the Urban Land Institute recognized Small's contributions to the real estate development industry with its Lifetime Achievement Award.

The Albert and Shirley Small Special Collections Library at dusk, with Alderman Library in the background to the right. Four-fifths of the 72,000-square-foot structure, completed in 2004, lie beneath the bricked plaza and landscaped light wells.

Complementing his vision for urban growth, Small has nurtured a lifelong interest in the development of the United States through his collecting of historical documents. He began acquiring maps and images of the nation's capital in his twenties and has been collecting ever since. In 2003, the Historical Society of Washington, D.C., mounted an exhibition and published a catalog featuring items from his extensive private collection.[1]

A member of the Washington Rare Book Group, the Manuscript Society, and Grolier Club of New York, Small's passion for historical collecting has led to gifts and involvements with many libraries and cultural heritage institutions, including the James Madison Council of the Library of Congress, the Foundation for the National Archives, the Life Guard of Historic Mount Vernon, the Tudor Place Foundation, and the Smithsonian Institution's National Museum of American History and National Museum of the American Indian. He is a trustee of the Folger Shakespeare Library, where he has played a vital role in enhancing the accessibility of its collections, most recently with the gift of an electronic kiosk where visitors can virtually "turn the page" of one of the library's First Folios. In addition, he serves on the boards of many other Washington-area cultural organizations, including the National Symphony Orchestra, the National Gallery of Art, Ford's Theatre, and the National Trust for the Humanities. Small is also an active trustee of the Aspen

Institute, an international nonprofit organization dedicated to fostering enlightened leadership and open-minded dialogue. The Woodrow Wilson International Center for Scholars of the Smithsonian Institution honored him with its corporate citizenship award in 2007.

Amid these broad commitments, Small has focused his primary philanthropic energies on his alma mater. Presently a trustee of the University of Virginia Foundation, he served on the university's Board of Visitors between 1992 and 2000, including a critical term as chair of the building committee. During that time, Small decided to give his Declaration of Independence collection to the university as a means of making it available both to students and the general public. Yet he wanted to do still more: to erect a new library building to showcase the collection along with the university's other special collections, notably holdings pertaining to American history, literature, and culture.

At the head of Thomas Jefferson's "Academical Village" stands the Rotunda, which served its original purpose as the university's main library for more than a century. But as the student body and grounds expanded, a larger library was sorely needed. In 1936, university president John Lloyd Newcomb secured assistance from the Public Works Administration to build a new library about a hundred yards west of the Rotunda. Named after

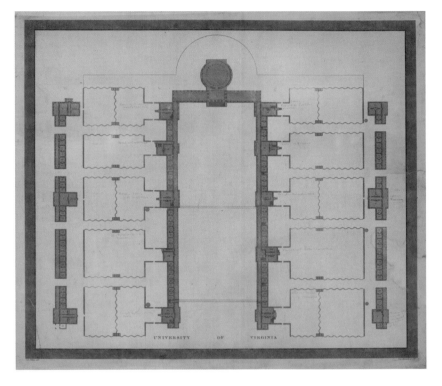

Newcomb's predecessor Edwin Alderman, it was formally dedicated during Final Exercises in June 1938. A simultaneous bequest from Detroit philanthropist and book collector Tracy W. McGregor led to the creation of a spacious, elegantly paneled room in Alderman Library to house rare book and manuscript collections and archives, including McGregor's exceptional collection of 12,500 volumes on American history and geography. In 1960, alumnus Clifton Waller Barrett began depositing his massive collection of American literature, comprising some 750,000 books, letters, and manuscripts covering nearly every American author between 1775 and 1950. By the 1970s, the university was formulating plans and fundraising for a separate edifice to house its burgeoning special collections.

Yet this dream needed Albert Small to waken the reality. The Albert and Shirley Small Special Collections Library, dedicated and opened in November 2004, represents the fruition of more than thirty years of striving and the culmination of a decade-long campaign "to keep the library at the head of the lawn." Other sites had been considered, but Small's brilliant proposal to create a partially underground facility adjacent to Alderman Library was adopted. The complex structure was designed by Hartman-Cox Architects of Washington, D.C., and erected over a three-year period. The surrounding landscaping was

In 1822, Peter Maverick made this engraving of the central grounds of the University of Virginia after original drawings by Thomas Jefferson. The Rotunda library stands at the head of Jefferson's "Academical Village," which consists of a terraced lawn flanked by symmetrical ranges of dormitory rooms and faculty pavilions connected by serpentine-walled gardens.

realized through a collaborative effort between the University Landscape Architect's Office and Oehme, van Sweden & Associates of Washington, D.C.

The Albert and Shirley Small Special Collections Library occupies 58,000 square feet of the 72,000-square-foot building, which also houses the Mary and David Harri-

son Institute for American, History, Literature, and Culture, dedicated to promoting and supporting use of the library's collections. A subterranean vault, built to the highest security and environmental standards and containing twelve miles of electronically controlled compact shelving, holds the 15.6 million manuscripts, 311,000 rare books, 213,000 photographs and prints, 9,000 reels of microfilm, 6,200 audio and video recordings, 3,000 maps, and thousands of pieces of realia that compose the university's special collections and archives. In addition to spaces for temporary exhibits, a permanent gallery offers visitors a unique opportunity to learn from and be inspired by highlights from the Albert H. Small Declaration of Independence Collection, which is fully available to researchers.

The reference area of the Albert and Shirley Small Special Collections Library provides public access to its extensive holdings of rare books and manuscripts pertaining to American history, literature, and culture.

Albert Small's interest in the Declaration of Independence grew out of his collecting of Washingtoniana and presidential letters. In time, he concentrated his efforts on collecting autograph documents of the Declaration's fifty-six signers, joining a long tradition of collectors who have attempted the arduous feat. Approaching the time of the centennial celebrations of Independence in 1876, sixteen private collectors and institutions had assembled complete sets of signers' autographs. By the mid-1950s, around the time that Small entered the fray, the number of complete sets had increased to forty, but thirty-three of these were claimed by institutional archives.[2] It had become increasingly difficult to obtain new materials on the market, making the quality and depth of Small's collection all the more extraordinary.

Most signers' letters in the collection date to 1776—among them, the only letter penned by a signer on 4 July 1776 recounting the events of that fateful day. Delaware delegate Caesar Rodney wrote to his brother, Thomas, about his arduous eighty-mile carriage ride from Dover to Philadelphia through "thunder and rain," arriving just in time to cast the deciding vote in "the matter of independence." "We have now Got through with the Whole of the declaration," he continued, "and Ordered it to be printed so that You will soon have the pleasure of seeing it. Hand bills of it will be printed and Sent to the Armies, Cities, Countys, Towns, &c. to be published or rather proclaimed in form." When Small

acquired this famous signer's autograph in 1989, he set a record for the highest price paid for a single letter at auction.

Several later letters from other signers preserve recollections of the congressional debates over the text of the Declaration and the process of its adoption. In a letter to Mercy Otis Warren (p. 69), the remarkable woman poet who was among the first to attempt a history of the Revolution, dated 2 February 1814, John Adams confides that fellow signer Thomas McKean was "mistaken in a day or two," explaining that "the final vote of Independance, [sic] after the last debate, was passed on the 2nd or third of July, and the Declaration prepared and signed on the 4th." "What are we to think of History?" he wonders, "When in less than 40 years such Diversities appear in the Memories of the living Persons who were witnesses." In another letter from 14 November 1825, Thomas Jefferson writes to his granddaughter Ellen Wayles Randolph Coolidge expressing sorrow that an ornate desk he had wanted to offer her as a wedding present had been lost at sea, adding that he would send as a substitute the portable writing box upon which he composed the Declaration. Although "plain," he commented, because "things acquire a superstitious value because of their connection with particular persons, surely a connection with the great Charter of our Independance [sic] may give a value to what has been associated with that." The original writing box is at the Smithsonian institution; an official replica is on display with the letter (p. 4).

The Small collection also contains some of the rarest signers' fragments: a fiscal document signed by Georgia delegate Button Gwinnett and the title page of a book

The Albert H. Small Declaration of Independence Gallery offers visitors a unique opportunity to view rare original printings of the Declaration and important autograph letters and documents from its fifty-six signers. A short documentary film provides historical background on the drafting, approval, publication, and influence of the Declaration, featuring items on display.

inscribed by South Carolina signer Thomas Lynch, both of whom died not long after signing the Declaration.

Alongside the signers' autographs stands a larger collection of broadside and newspaper printings of the Declaration and related documents, images and books that Small has gathered piece by piece. Some of these have passed through the hands of other notable twentieth-century collectors, such as Benjamin Chew and Carrie Estelle Doheny.

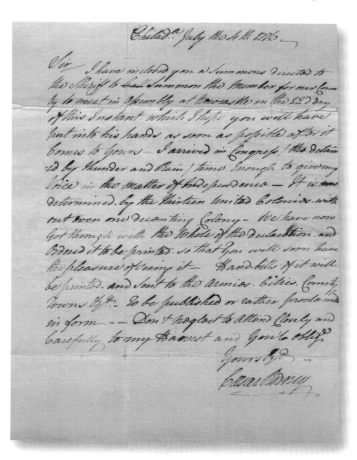

In this famous letter, Delaware delegate Caesar Rodney recounts his dramatic arrival in Congress on 2 July 1776, "tho detained by thunder and Rain," just in time to break the split in his delegation and seal the critical vote in favor of independence. Over the next two days, Congress debated the text of the Declaration, approving a final version for publication on 4 July.

The Small collection presently includes original examples of six of the eighteen contemporary broadside or single-sheet printings of the Declaration believed to have been issued in 1776, a proportion matched only by Houghton Library at Harvard University and the Library of Congress.[3] The collection is further distinguished for possessing one of the most pristine of the twenty-five known surviving examples of the first printing by John Dunlap of Philadelphia (p. viii), made only hours after the final text was approved by Congress on the afternoon of 4 July. Its provenance can be securely traced to George Washington's personal secretary, Tobias Lear, making it likely that it belonged to the great general himself.[4]

Other contemporary broadsides in the collection are also extremely rare. On or about 9 July, just after a copy of the Dunlap broadside sent to Washington was read to his troops in New York City and patriots had torn down the statue of George III on Bowling Green, Hugh Gaine, publisher of the *New-York Gazzette and the Weekly Mercury*, printed his own broadside version of the text. The only other surviving example is held by the New-York Historical Society. In addition, the Small collection contains the only extant copy of a two-column broadside of the Declaration discovered in Kingston, New York, in the 1940s.

The collection also contains more than a dozen of the earliest newspaper printings and notices concerning the Declaration: the first printing of the complete text in any newspaper (6 July *Pennsylvania Evening Post*, p. xvi), the first announcement of the Declaration in Virginia (19 July *Virginia Gazette*, p. 59), and the first newspaper printing in Britain (15/17 August *London Chronicle*, p. 33). So, too, may be found the first appearance of the Declaration in a book, Samuel Bryan's *Genuine Principles of the Ancient Saxon, or English Constitution*, published in Philadelphia by Robert Bell only days after the first broadsides and newspapers circulated the text.

Inspired by the revival of patriotic sentiment after the War of 1812 and a growing awareness of the passing of the signers' generation, several engravers produced decorative facsimiles of the engrossed copy of the Declaration, which by then was suffering damage

In CONGRESS, July 4, 1776.

A DECLARATION

By the REPRESENTATIVES of the

UNITED STATES OF AMERICA,

In GENERAL CONGRESS ASSEMBLED.

WHEN in the Course of human Events, it becomes necessary for one People to dissolve the Political Bands which have connected them with another, and to assume among the Powers of the Earth, the separate and equal Station to which the Laws of Nature and Nature's God entitle them, a decent Respect to the Opinions of Mankind requires that they should declare the Causes which impel them to the Separation.

We hold these Truths to be self-evident, that all Men are created equal, that they are endowed by their Creator with certain unalienable Rights, that among these are Life, Liberty and the Pursuit of Happiness.—That to secure these Rights, Governments are instituted among Men, deriving their just Powers from the Consent of the Governed, that whenever any Form of Government becomes destructive of these Ends, it is the Right of the People to alter or to abolish it, and to institute new Government, laying its Foundation on such Principles, and organizing its Powers in such Form, as to them shall seem most likely to effect their Safety and Happiness. Prudence, indeed will dictate that Governments long established should not be changed for light and transient Causes; and accordingly all Experience hath shewn, that Mankind are more disposed to suffer, while Evils are sufferable, than to right themselves by abolishing the Forms to which they are accustomed. But when a long Train of Abuses and Usurpations, pursuing invariably the same Object, evinces a Design to reduce them under absolute Despotism, it is their Right, it is their Duty, to throw off such Government, and to provide new Guards for their future Security. Such has been the patient Sufferance of these Colonies; and such is now the Necessity which constrains them to alter their former Systems of Government. The History of the present King of Great-Britain is a History of repeated Injuries and Usurpations, all having in direct Object the Establishment of an absolute Tyranny over these States. To prove this, let Facts be submitted to a candid World.

He has refused his Assent to Laws, the most wholesome and necessary for the public Good.

He has forbidden his Governors to pass Laws of immediate and pressing Importance, unless suspended in their Operation till his Assent should be obtained; and when so suspended, he has utterly neglected to attend to them.

He has refused to pass other Laws for the Accommodation of large Districts of People, unless those People would relinquish the Right of Representation in the Legislature, a Right inestimable to them, and formidable to Tyrants only.

He has called together Legislative Bodies at Places unusual, uncomfortable, and distant from the Depository of their public Records, for the sole Purpose of fatiguing them into Compliance with his Measures.

He has dissolved Representative Houses repeatedly, for opposing with manly Firmness his Invasions on the Rights of the People.

He has refused for a long Time, after such Dissolutions, to cause others to be elected; whereby the Legislative Powers, incapable of Annihilation, have returned to the People at large for their exercise; the State remaining in the mean time exposed to all the Dangers of Invasion from without, and Convulsions within.

He has endeavoured to prevent the Population of these States; for that Purpose obstructing the Laws for Naturalization of Foreigners; refusing to pass others to encourage their Migrations hither, and raising the Conditions of new Appropriations of Lands.

He has obstructed the Administration of Justice, by refusing his Assent to Laws for establishing Judiciary Powers.

He has made Judges dependent on his Will alone, for the Tenure of their Offices, and the Amount and Payment of their Salaries.

He has erected a Multitude of new Offices, and sent hither Swarms of Officers to harrass our People, and eat out their Subsistence.

He has kept among us, in Times of Peace, Standing Armies, without the Consent of our Legislatures.

He has affected to render the Military independent of and superior to the Civil Power.

He has combined with others to subject us to a Jurisdiction foreign to our Constitution, and unacknowledged by our Laws; giving his Assent to their Acts of pretended Legislation:

For quartering large Bodies of armed Troops among us:

For protecting them, by a mock Trial, from Punishment for any Murders which they should commit on the Inhabitants of these States:

For cutting off our Trade with all Parts of the World:

For imposing Taxes on us without our Consent:

For depriving us, in many Cases, of the Benefits of Trial by Jury:

For transporting us beyond Seas to be tried for pretended Offences:

For abolishing the free System of English Laws in a neighbouring Province, establishing therein an arbitrary Government, and enlarging its Boundaries, so as to render it at once an Example and fit Instrument for introducing the same absolute Rule into these Colonies:

For taking away our Charters, abolishing our most valuable Laws, and altering fundamentally the Forms of our Governments:

For suspending our own Legislatures, and declaring themselves invested with Power to legislate for us in all Cases whatsoever.

He has abdicated Government here, by declaring us out of his Protection and waging War against us.

He has plundered our Seas, ravaged our Coasts, burnt our Towns, and destroyed the Lives of our People.

He is, at this Time, transporting large Armies of foreign Mercenaries to compleat the Works of Death, Desolation and Tyranny, already begun with Circumstances of Cruelty and Perfidy, scarcely paralleled in the most barbarous Ages, and totally unworthy the Head of a civilized Nation.

He has constrained our fellow Citizens taken Captive on the high Seas to bear Arms against their Country, to become the Executioners of their Friends and Brethren, or to fall themselves by their Hands.

He has excited Domestic Insurrections amongst us, and has endeavoured to bring on the Inhabitants of our Frontiers, the merciless Indian Savages, whose known Rule of Warfare, is an undistinguished Destruction, of all Ages, Sexes and Conditions.

In every Stage of these Oppressions we have petitioned for Redress, in the most humble Terms: Our repeated Petitions have been answered only by repeated Injury. A Prince, whose Character is thus marked by every Act which may define a Tyrant, is unfit to be the Ruler of a free People.

Nor have we been wanting in Attentions to our British Brethren. We have warned them from Time to Time of Attempts by their Legislature to extend an unwarrantable Jurisdiction over us. We have reminded them of the Circumstances of our Emigration and Settlement here. We have appealed to their native Justice and Magnanimity, and we have conjured them by the Ties of our common Kindred to disavow these Usurpations, which would inevitably interrupt our Connections and Correspondence. They too have been deaf to the Voice of Justice and of Consanguinity. We must, therefore, acquiesce in the Necessity which denounces our Separation, and hold them, as we hold the rest of Mankind, Enemies in War, in Peace, Friends.

We, therefore, the Representatives of the UNITED STATES OF AMERICA, in GENERAL CONGRESS assembled, appealing to the Supreme Judge of the World for the Rectitude of our Intentions, do, in the Name and by the Authority of the good People of these Colonies, solemnly Publish and Declare, That these United Colonies are, and of Right ought to be, FREE AND INDEPENDENT STATES; that they are absolved from all Allegiance to the British Crown, and that all political Connection between them and the State of Great-Britain, is and ought to be totally dissolved; and that as FREE AND INDEPENDENT STATES, they have full Power to levy War, conclude Peace, contract Alliances, establish Commerce, and to do all other Acts and Things which INDEPENDENT STATES may of right do. And for the Support of this Declaration, with a firm Reliance on the Protection of divine Providence we mutually pledge to each other our Lives, our Fortunes, and our sacred Honor.

Signed by ORDER and in BEHALF of the CONGRESS,

JOHN HANCOCK, President.

ATTEST.

CHARLES THOMSON, SECRETARY.

NEW-YORK: Printed by HUGH GAINE, in Hanover-Square.

Many localties in the new United States printed copies of the Declaration in the weeks following its first publication by John Dunlap in Philadelphia on 5 July 1776. This unique surviving example of an early broadside was discovered in an old house near Kingston, New York, in the 1940s.

LEFT: New-York Gazette *publisher Hugh Gaine printed this rare broadside of the Declaration shortly after General George Washington had the text read to the troops defending the city on 9 July 1776. Two months later Gaine fled to New Jersey with his family and one of his presses, but he returned in November, having relinquished the patriot cause and becoming a mouthpiece for British and loyalist positions.*

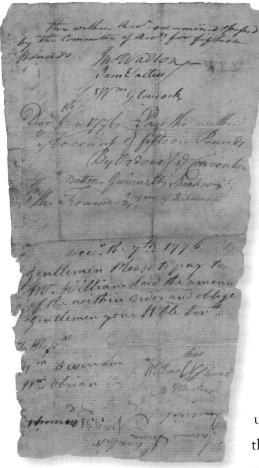

Experts agree that autographs of Button Gwinnett are the most difficult of the signers to obtain because he died from wounds suffered in a pistol duel with a political rival on 19 May 1777. Of the forty-seven known surviving autographs of Gwinnett, only seven, including the engrossed Declaration and this fragment of a fiscal document, date to 1776.

OPPOSITE: *This commemorative engraving was produced for Philadelphia's 1876 centennial exhibition. It features the text of the Declaration in an outline of the Liberty Bell, which tradition held was sounded to gather citizens for its first public reading. Surrounding vignettes depict the exhibition grounds; Independence Hall and Carpenters' Hall, where the first two continental congresses met; and seals for all thirty-eight states at the time, including Colorado, which had just been admitted to the union.*

from repeated exhibitions. The Small collection not only contains examples of all of these facsimiles, but also some intriguing related items, such as the subscription book in which Benjamin Owen Tyler recorded the distribution of copies of his ornamental engraving to Thomas Jefferson, James Madison, John Quincy Adams, and other prominent figures (p. 63).

In 1820 Congress authorized an official and exact facsimile of the engrossed Declaration to be made. Secretary of State John Quincy Adams commissioned William J. Stone to make the copperplate engraving, which reportedly took a full three years. Stone printed two hundred copies on fine vellum, one of which was given to the Marquis de Lafayette for his service in the Revolution when he visited the United States in 1824. He considered it a prized possession. When he died, it was hanging in his bedchamber. It now hangs in the permanent *Declaring Independence* exhibition gallery.

A comprehensive series of later printings of the Declaration shows how the document came to be revered during successive decades of the nineteenth century through the first centenary of Independence in 1876. Some elaborately bordered and decorated, some exacting in their replication of the signers' autographs, some creating pictures from the very words of the Declaration, some printed on silk (p. 66) or linen as parade scarves and banners—all bear witness to the transformation of a potent political statement into the iconic expression of rights and freedoms that the Declaration has come to symbolize.

A series of portraits of forty-nine of the signers (p. 42ff) bears close resemblance to those in a painting titled *Congress Voting Independence* that has been attributed to English artist Robert Edge Pine, who came to the United States around 1783 to paint the eminent figures of the American Revolution. In addition, there are numerous prints modeled after John Trumbull's well-known painting (p. xvii) depicting the drafting committee's presentation of the Declaration to the Continental Congress.

In all, the collection currently contains more than 350 carefully selected pieces brought together over the course of more than fifty years by Albert Small's persistent efforts to capture the personalities and legacies of the founders of our nation.

Notes

1 James M. Goode and Laura Bird Schiavo, *Washington Images: Rare Maps and Prints from the Albert H. Small Collection* (Washington, DC, 2004).

2 See Joseph E. Fields, "Completed Sets of the Signers of the Declaration of Independence." *Autograph Collector's Journal* (January, 1951), 15–19, and an updated report: "A Census: Sets of Signers of the Declaration of Independence," *Manuscripts* (Spring 1956), 149–52.

3 Michael J. Walsh, "Contemporary Broadside Editions of the Declaration of Independence." *Harvard Library Bulletin 3* (1949): 31–43. The Small Collection presently includes examples of Walsh 1, 4, 6, 7, 10, 13.

4 Joseph E. Fields, *George Washington's Copy of John Dunlap's First Printing of the Declaration of Independence in the Albert Harrison Small Collection, Washington, D.C.* (Williamsburg, VA, 1996).

About the Authors

DAVID ARMITAGE is Lloyd C. Blankfein Professor of History at Harvard University, where he teaches intellectual history and international history. He was educated at Cambridge University and Princeton University, and has held teaching and research positions in Britain, the United States, and Australia. He is the author of *The Ideological Origins of the British Empire* (2000), *Greater Britain, 1516-1776: Essays in Atlantic History* (2004) and *The Declaration of Independence: A Global History* (2007), and the editor of six books, including *The British Atlantic World, 1500-1800* (with Michael J. Braddick, 2002). In 2006, the National Maritime Museum in London awarded him its Caird Medal in recognition of his contributions to historical studies.

CHRISTIAN Y. DUPONT has been Director of the Albert and Shirley Small Special Collections Library at the University of Virginia since 2006. He previously held administrative and curatorial positions in special collections at Syracuse University and the University of Notre Dame. He has published and lectured on nineteenth-century library history and curated numerous exhibitions. He holds a doctorate in the history of Christianity from the University of Notre Dame and a master of information science from Indiana University.

PAULINE MAIER is William Rand Kenan, Jr., Professor of American History at the Massachusetts Institute of Technology. She is the author of *American Scripture, Making the Declaration of Independence*, which appeared on the *New York Times Book Review* editors' choice list of the eleven best books, fiction and nonfiction, of 1997, and *The Old Revolutionaries: Political Lives in the Age of Samuel Adams* (1980). She has also contributed to textbooks on American history and appeared on several programs for the History Channel and PBS. She is presently writing a narrative history of the ratification of the Constitution under contract with Simon and Schuster.

DAVID MCCULLOUGH, author of the *New York Times* number one national bestseller *1776*, is twice winner of the Pulitzer Prize for his historical biographies *John Adams* and *Truman*, as well as a two-time winner of the National Book Award. An editor, essayist, teacher, lecturer, he is also a familiar presence on public television, as host of *Smithsonian World* and *The American Experience*, and as narrator of numerous documentaries, including *The Civil War*. In December 2006, McCullough was awarded the Presidential Medal of Freedom, the nations's highest civilian award, in recognition of his "lifelong efforts to document the people, places, and events that have shaped America."

ROBERT M. S. MCDONALD is associate professor of history at the United States Military Academy. A graduate of the University of Virginia and Oxford University, he earned his Ph.D. at the University of North Carolina at Chapel Hill. He has authored articles and essays for publications such as *Southern Cultures*, *The Historian*, and *The Jouranl of the Early Republic*, and is editor of *Thomas Jefferson's Military Academy: Founding West Point* (2004). He is completing a book to be titled *Confounding Father: Thomas Jefferson and the Politics of Personality*.

JUSTICE SANDRA DAY O'CONNOR became the first woman appointed to the United States Supreme Court following her nomination by President Ronald Reagan in 1981. During her 25-year tenure, she often cast the deciding vote in cases concerning affirmative action, abortion, states rights, and the separation of church and state. Justice O'Connor retired from the Supreme Court in 2006. She had previously served on the Arizona Court of Appeals and Maricopa County Superior Court and as Arizona State Senator and Assistant Attorney General.

PETER S. ONUF is Thomas Jefferson Foundation Professor of History at the University of Virginia. He has written extensively on sectionalism, federalism, and political economy, with a particular emphasis on the political thought of Thomas Jefferson. His books include *The Mind of Thomas Jefferson* (2007), *Jeffersonian America* (with Leonard J. Sadosky, 2002), and *Jefferson's Empire: The Language of American Nationhood* (2000). He is also editor with Jan Lewis of *Sally Hemings and Thomas Jefferson: History, Memory, and Civic Culture* (1999) and *Jeffersonian Legacies* (1993). With his brother, political theorist Nicholas G. Onuf, he collaborated on *Nations, Markets, and War: Modern History and the American Civil War* (2006).

❖

ROBERT G. PARKINSON is Assistant Professor of History at the College of William & Mary and postdoctoral fellow at the College's Omohundro Institute for Early American History and Culture, where he is working on a book on race and the American Revolution. His publications have appeared in the *William & Mary Quarterly* and *Virginia Magazine of History and Biography*. He has taught at Shepherd College and holds degrees from the University of Virginia and the University of Tennessee.

Photograph and Illustration Credits

All items are from the Albert H. Small Declaration of Independence Collection unless otherwise noted. Items identified as McGregor are from the Tracy W. McGregor Library of American History, University of Virginia Library.

Still images from *Declaring Independence* are from a short documentary film for the Albert H. Small Declaration of Independence gallery produced by Bill Reifenberger, Silverthorn Films, and narrated by Michael Beschloss, copyright 2004 by the Rector and Visitors of the University of Virginia.

Portraits of some of the Declaration signers are reproduced from plates from an extra-illustrated copy of William Brotherhead, *The Centennial Book of the Signers, Being Fac-Simile Letters of Each Signer of the Declaration of Independence, Illustrated with One Hundred Engravings, of Portraits, Views, Etc., Including Thirteen Original Designs, Colored by Hand, with a Historical Monograph and a History of the Centennial Exhibition* (Philadelphia, J.M. Stoddart & Co., 1872 [1875]).

Unless otherwise noted, all images were scanned by the University of Virginia Library digital services unit. Special thanks go to Christina Deane, Kristy Haney, and the many students who performed the scanning and quality control. Additional thanks are due Mercy Quintos and George Riser for image research.

The editors wish to gratefully acknowledge the research and writing assistance of doctoral students James Cocola, Scott Harrop, and Dana Stefanelli, as well as the work of Jay Fliegelman (1949–2007), whose *Declaring Independence: Jefferson, Natural Language and the Culture of Performance* (Stanford, 1993) inspired the title of this volume.

vii: Photograph of David McCullough courtesy of David McCullough and William B. McCullough, photographer.

viii: *In Congress, July 4, 1776. A Declaration by the Representatives of the United States of America, in General Congress Assembled. ...* (Philadelphia, Printed by John Dunlap, [1776]), 48 x 35.5 cm. [KF4506 .A1 1776]

ix: Reenactor reading the Declaration. Still image from *Declaring Independence* (see introductory note).

x: Thomas Paine, *Common Sense ...* (Boston, Re-printed, and sold by Edes & Gill and T. & J. Fleet, 1776). [McGregor A 1776 .P352] • Engraving of Thomas Paine. Frontispiece to Thomas Paine, *Rights of Man* (London, Printed for H.D. Symonds, Paternoster-Row, 1792), first of seven titles by Paine in pamphlet volume. [JC 177 .C21 1792c no.1] Gift of Richard Maass.

xi: Reenactment of Dunlap printing the Declaration. Still image from *Declaring Independence*.

xiii: Map of Boston and Bunker Hill from James Murray, *An Impartial History of the Present War in America* (London, Printed for R. Baldwin [et al. 1778–1780]). [McGregor A 1778 .M87]

xiv: Portrait of King George III. Frontispiece to John Andrews, *History of the War with America, France, Spain, and Holland ...* (London, J. Fielding, 1785–1786). [McGregor A 1785 .A537 v.1] • Battle of Bunker Hill. Engraved plate from George Cockings, *The American War, a poem, in six books ...* (London, Printed by W. Richardson for the author, 1781). [Barrett PS586 .Z92 .C63 A5 1781] Gift of C. Waller Barrett • Thomas Paine, *Common Sense ...* (Boston, Re-printed, and sold by Edes & Gill and T. & J. Fleet, 1776). [McGregor A 1776 .P352]

xv: Portrait of Richard Henry Lee. ([Philadelphia?], [before 1831]), engraved by P. Maverick and J. Longacre after a drawing taken by Longacre from an original, 10.2 x 8.3 cm. [MSS 12615] • "Drafting the Declaration of Independence" (New York: Johnson, Fry & Co., Publishers, 1867), hand-colored engraving after a painting by Alonzo

Chappel, image 18 x 14 cm. on sheet 28 x 21 cm. [KF 4506 .A2 D73 1867] • Samuel Holland, *The Seat of Action, between the British and American Forces; Or, An Authentic Plan of the Western Part of Long Island, with the Engagement of the 27th August 1776 between the King's Forces and the Americans ...*(London, Printed for Robt. Sayer and Jno. Bennett, Map and Sea Chartsellers, No. 53 Fleet Street, as the Act directs, 22d Octr. 1776), 44 x 39 cm. [G3802 .L6 S3 1776 .H6] Gift of Seymour I. Schwartz • "The Declaration of Independence of the United States of America, July 4th, 1776" ([Philadelphia (94 Walnut St., Philada, published at J.T. Bowen's Lithographic Establishment, [between 1838 and 1844]), hand-colored lithograph by Ralph Trembley after a painting by John Trumbull, 50 x 70 cm. [KF4506 .A2 T78 1838c]

xvi: Portrait of Caesar Rodney after Robert Edge Pine (oil on board, no date), 25 x 22.5 cm. [MSS 12130] • Reenactment of horseback rider delivering Declaration. Still image from *Declaring Independence* (see introductory note). • Reenactor reading the Declaration. Still image from *Declaring Independence* (see introductory note). • *In Congress, July 4, 1776. A Declaration by the Representatives of the United States of America, in General Congress Assembled. ...* (Philadelphia, Printed by John Dunlap. [1776]), 48 x 35.5 cm. [KF4506 .A1 1776] • *The Pennsylvania Evening Post* (Philadelphia, Benjamin Towne, July 6, 1776). [KF4506 .A1 1776a]

xvii: "Pulling down the Statue of George III by the "Sons of Freedom," at the Bowling Green, City of New York, July 1776" ([New York, published by John C. McRae, ca. 1876]), engraved and etched image 52 x 77 cm. on sheet 65 x 89 cm. [KF4506 .A3 P85 1876]• Reenactment of the Second Continental Congress. Still image from *Declaring Independence* (see introductory note). • *In Congress, July 4, 1776. The Unanimous Declaration of the Thirteen United States of America* ([Washington, D.C.], engraved by W.I. Stone for the Dept. of State by order of J.Q. Adams, Sect. of State, July 4th, 1823, [1823]), printed on vellum, formerly owned by the Marquis de Lafayette, 84 x 68 cm. [KF4506 .A1 1823]

xviii: "A Fac Simile of the Original Rough Draft of the Declaration of Independence" from *Brother Jonathan* (New York, Wilson and Co., 4 July 1848). [KF4506 .A1 1848]

1: Portrait engraving of Thomas Jefferson from William Brotherhead, *The Centennial Book of the Signers* (see introductory note). [KF4506 .Z8 C45 1875b]

2: *Fac simile de quelques signatures de l'acte d'Indépéndance*, presumably a plate removed from a book published in Paris after 1800, 21 x 13 cm. [KF4506 .A2 E8 1800]

3: *"The Drafting of the Declaration of Independence"* after a painting by Jean Leon Gerome Ferris (Philadelphia, Dr. Jayne's Family Medicines, 1909), picture postcard, 14 x 9 cm. [KF4506 .A3 F47 1909]

4: Portrait of Thomas Jefferson by Charles Peale Polk (Oil on canvas, 1799[?]), 64 x 49cm. [MSS 8149] Gift of Mr. and Mrs. J. William Middendorf II. Photograph by Tom Cogill. • Replica of Thomas Jefferson's writing box, Smithsonian Institution (2003). [MSS 12623] Photograph by Tom Cogill.

5: *Declaration of Rights, and Plan of Government for the State of New-Hampshire* (Exeter, Printed by Zechariah Fowle, 1779), 39 x 31 cm. [KF4506 .A3 N48 1779]

6: *The Declaration Committee* (New York, Currier & Ives, 1876), hand-colored lithograph, 31 x 41 cm. [KF4506 .A2 C87 1876]

7: Matthäus Albrecht Lotter, *A Plan of the City and Environs of Philadelphia* ([Augsburg?], M.A. Lotter, 1777), hand-colored map, 60 x 46 cm. [KF3506 .A2 L67 1777]

8: Reenactment of nailing a copy of the Declaration to a door. Still image from *Declaring Independence* (see introductory note).

9: John Russell Pope, competition drawing for the Jefferson Memorial in Washington, D.C. (29 March 1938), 61.6 x 138.5 cm. [MSS 8731] Gift of Congressman Howard Worth Smith.

10: "Pulling down the Statue of George III by the 'Sons of Freedom,' at the Bowling Green, City of New York, July 1776" ([New York, published by John C. McRae, ca. 1876]), engraved and etched image 52 x 77 cm. on sheet 65 x 89 cm. [KF4506 .A3 P85 1876]

11: Portrait of King George III. Frontispiece to John Andrews, *History of the War with America, France, Spain, and Holland ...* (London, J. Fielding, 1785-1786). [McGregor A 1785 .A537 v.1]

12: Arthur Middleton, autograph letter to William Henry Drayton, 14 September 1776 [MSS 12609] • Portrait of Arthur Middleton. ([Philadelphia?], [before 1861]), engraved by J. Longacre after a drawing taken by T. Middleton from a family picture by Benjamin West. [MSS 12609]

13: William Hamilton, *The Manner in which the American Colonies Declared Themselves Independant of the King of England, Throughout the Different Provinces, on July 4, 1776* ([London, Alexander Hogg, 1783?]), 39 x 23 cm. [KF4506 .A2 H25 1783]

14: Resolution by town of Danvers, Massachusetts, 26 August 1779. (Danvers, Printed by E. Russell, at his Printing-Office, near the Bell-Tavern, [1779]), 13 x 32 cm. [KF4506 .A3 D27 1997]

15: Oliver Wolcott, autograph letter signed to Roger Newberry, 4 June 1776. [MSS 12565] • Portrait of Oliver Wolcott after Robert Edge Pine (oil on board, no date), 25 x 22.5 cm. [MSS 12130]

16: "The Bloody Massacre Perpetrated in King-Street Boston on March 5th 1770 by a Party of the 29th Regt." from *The Paul Revere Portfolio: Works that Changed America ... A Unique Portfolio of Engravings Taken from the Original Copperplates Hand Engraved by Patriot and Silversmith Paul Revere at the Time of the American Revolution ...* ([Boston, Haley & Steele Gallery], 2005) 35 x 45 cm. [KF4506 .R48 2005]

19: Thomas Gage proclamation. *By His Excellency, the Hon. Thomas Gage, Esq. Governor, and Commander in Chief, in and over His Majesty's Province of Massachusetts-Bay, and Vice-Admiral of the Same: a Proclamation* ([Boston?, Margaret Draper?, 1775]) 50 x 40 cm. [KF4506 .M3 1775]

20: "Drafting the Declaration of Independence" (New York: Johnson, Fry & Co., Publishers, 1857), hand-colored engraving after a painting by Alonzo Chappel, image 18 x 14 cm. on sheet 28 x 21 cm. [KF 4506 .A2 D73 1857]

21: Thomas Jefferson, *A Summary View of the Rights of British America, Set Forth in Some Resolutions Intended for the Inspection of the Present Delegates of the People of Virginia, Now in Convention* (Williamsburg [VA], printed by Clementina Rind, [1774]) [E211 .M45 1774b no.1] Rare Book Collection.

22: Matthäus Albrecht Lotter, *A Plan of the City and Environs of Philadelphia* ([Augsburg?], M.A. Lotter, 1777), hand-colored map, 60 x 46 cm. [KF3506 .A2 L67 1777]

23: Portrait of Ezra Stiles. Frontispiece to Ezra Stiles, *A History of Three of the Judges of King Charles I …* (Hartford, printed by Elisha Babcock, 1794) [McGregor A 1794 .S75]

24: Thomas Jefferson, autograph letter signed to Samuel Smith, 17 October 1800. [MSS 12613]

26: Portrait of Richard Henry Lee from William Brotherhead, *The Centennial Book of the Signers* (see introductory note). [KF4506 .Z8 C45 1875b]

27: Tombstone of Thomas Jefferson, Monticello, Virginia. Photograph courtesy of Monticello/ Thomas Jefferson Foundation.

28: President Abraham Lincoln, *Proclamation of Emancipation* (Philadelphia, L. Franklin Smith, 1865), 62 x 47 cm. [KF4506 .A3 U6 1865]

30: Joseph A. Arnold, *Independence Declared 1776* ([Boston], Joseph A. Arnold, 1839), lithograph, 72 x 48 cm. [KF4506 .A2 A75 1839]

31 : Jean Nicolas Démeunier, *L'Amérique Indépendante, ou les différentes constitutions des treize provinces qui se sont érigées en républiques, sous le nom d'États-Unis de l'Amérique* (Ghent, P. F. de Goesin, 1790) [McGregor A 1790 .D454]

32: John Lind, *An Answer to the Declaration of the American Congress* (London, printed for T. Cadell in the Strand, J. Walter, Charing-Cross, and T. Sewell, near the Royal Exchange, 1776) [KF4506 .L55 1776] • Portrait of Jeremy Bentham. Frontispiece to *Principles of Legislation: From the Ms. of Jeremy Bentham* (Boston, Wells and Lilly; New York, G. & C. & H. Carvill; [etc., etc.], 1830) [Barrett PS2459 .N28 P7 1830] Gift of C. Waller Barrett.

33: *London Chronicle* (London, Sold by J. Wilkie, 15/17 August 1776) [KF4506 .A1 1776k]

34: Portrait of Lord Byron. Frontispiece to George Gordon Byron, *The Works of Lord Byron* (Philadelphia, J. Lippincott & Co., 1865) [PR4351 .L3 1865] Gift of William C. Davis.

35: South Carolina. Convention (1860–1862). *Declaration of Independence of the State of South Carolina, in convention, at the city of Charleston, December 20, 1860.* (Charleston (3 Broad Street), Evans & Cogswell, [1860?]) 51 x 30 cm. [KF4506 .A3 S68 1860]

36: United Estates of Labor, Agriculture, Commerce, the Mechanic and Liberal Arts. *The United Estates of Labor, Agriculture, Commerce, the Mechanic and Liberal Arts, and all other professions and occupations of life, in Congress Assembled, promulgate the following unanimous Declaration of Temperance.* (Boston, Engraved by Devereux & Brown and printed by Wm. White and H.P. Lewis, Printers, Spring Lane, [between 1842 and 1844]) 71 x 53 cm. [KF4506 .A3 U58 1842]

38: *Dunlap's Pennsylvania Packet, or the General Advertiser* (Philadelphia, J. Dunlap, 22 July 1776) [KF4506 .A1 1776k]

41: Robert Edge Pine, completed by Edward Savage, "Congress Voting Independence" (oil on canvas, [1784-1801]) 50.2 cm x 67.3 cm. [HSP.1904.1] Courtesy of the Atwater Kent Museum of Philadelphia, Historical Society of Pennsylvania Collection.

42–56: Except as noted below, all portraits in the Gallery of the Signers are from undated oil on board paintings after Robert Edge Pine, approximately 25 x 22.5 cm. [MSS 12130]

45: Charles Willson Peale, portrait of Benjamin Franklin (1785), oil on canvas, 58.7 x 48.4 cm. [1912.14.2] Courtesy of the Pennsylvania Academy of the Fine Arts. • James Bogle, portrait of Elbridge Gerry (1861), oil on canvas, after a drawing by John Vanderlyn, 77.5 x 65.5 cm. [INDE 14054] Courtesy of Independence National Historical Park.

46: Potrait of Samuel Huntington from William Brotherhead, *The Centennial Book of the Signers* (see introductory note). [KF4506 .Z8 C45 1875b]

53: Portrait of Lewis Morris from William Brotherhead, *The Centennial Book of the Signers* (see introductory note). [KF4506 .Z8 C45 1875b]

55: Miniature portrait of James Smith by an unknown artist, circa 1760, watercolor on board, 2.9 x 2.5 cm. [1154] Courtesy of the R.W. Norton Art Gallery, Shreveport, LA.

56: Portrait of Matthew Thornton by Nahum Ball Onthank (1823–1888), circa 1850–1880, oil on canvas, approximately 61 x 51 cm. [1925.17] Courtesy of the New Hampshire Historical Society. • Portrait of George Walton from William Brotherhead, *The Centennial Book of the Signers* (see introductory note). [KF4506 .Z8 C45 1875b]

57: Benjamin Owen Tyler, Declaration of Independence facsimile subscription book, 1815–1818. [MSS 12143]

58: *The Pennsylvania Evening Post* (Philadelphia, Benjamin Towne, July 6, 1776). [KF4506 .A1 1776a]

59: *The Virginia Gazette* (Williamsburg, VA, Alexander Purdie, 19 July 1776) [Newspaper Virginia Williamsburg]

60: *In Congress, July 4, 1776. A Declaration by the Representatives of the United States of America, in General Congress Assembled …* (Newport [RI], printed by S. Southwick, 13 June [i.e., July] 1776), 52 x 40 cm. [KF4506 .A1 1776b]

61: *In Congress, July 4, 1776. A Declaration by the Representatives of the United States of America, in General Congress Assembled …* (Salem, Massachusetts-Bay, printed by E. Russell, by order of authority, 1776), 51 x 41 cm. [KF4506 .A1 1776ab]

62: *In Congress, July 4th, 1776. The Unanimous Declaration of the Thirteen United States of America. … Copied from the Original Declaration of Independence in the Department of State … Engraved by Peter Maverick, New Jersey* (Washington [DC], published by Benjamin Owen Tyler, 1818), 78 x 61 cm. [KF4506 .A1 1818b]

63: Benjamin Owen Tyler. *Subscription book for facsimile Declaration of Independence, 1815–1818.* [MSS 12143]

64: *In Congress, July 4th, 1776. The Unanimous Declaration of the Thirteen United States of America, … Entered According to Act of Congress the 4th day of November, 1818* ([Philadelphia], James Porter for John Binns, 1819), 89 x 62 cm. [KF4506 .A1 1818]

65: John Adams, autograph letter signed to John Binns, 20 September 1819. [MSS 12576-c]

66: *In Congress, July 4th, 1776. The Unanimous Declaration of the Thirteen United States of America.* ([Lyon, France, by H. Brunet, after 1820]), lithograph, adaptation from a design published by William Woodruff in 1819, 71 x 53 cm. [KF4506 .A1 1830b]

67: *In Congress, July 4, 1776. The Unanimous Declaration of the Thirteen United States of America* ([Washington, D.C.], engraved by W.I. Stone for the Dept. of State by order of J.Q. Adams, Sect. of State, July 4th, 1823, [1823]), printed on vellum, formerly owned by the Marquis de Lafayette, 84 x 68 cm. [KF4506 .A1 1823]

68: Mercy Otis Warren, autograph letter signed to Elbridge Gerry, 29 July 1805, with draft reply from Gerry to Warren dated 20 August 1805 on the verso of the address leaf. [MSS 12578-a]

69: John Adams, autograph letter signed to Mercy Otis Warren, 2 February 1814. [MSS 12576-a]

70: *The Declaration of Independence, Drawn with a Steel Pen by R. Morris Swander and Engraved (Fac Simile) by P.S. Duval & Son, Philada.; This Allegorical Portrait of Washington Respectfully Dedicated to the Christian Commission's of the United States by the Publishers* (Philadelphia, published by the Art Publishing Association of Philadelphia, Swander, Bishop & Cos., 1865), image 54 x 41 cm. [KF4506 .A1 1865]

71: John A. Fuller, *Freedom's Footsteps, the Thirteen United Colonies in Order as They Adopted the Constitution* (Nevada County, CA, 1866), pen and ink, colored, 66 x 50cm. [MSS 13936] Manuscript design for lithograph by W. Vallance Gray, Lith., printed by E. Fletcher, published by John A. Fuller (San Francisco, CA, 1866) [KF4506 .A1 1866]

72: Albert H. Small. Photograph by Tom Cogill. • "Declaring Independence" exhibition, Albert H. Small Declaration of Independence gallery. Photograph by Riggs Ward.

73: Thomas Jefferson, southern elevation of the Rotunda (1819), ink on paper, 22 x 18.5 cm. [MSS 8740, N-328]

74: Albert and Shirley Small Special Collections Library at dusk. Photograph by Bryan Becker.

75: Plan of the University of Virginia (1825), drawn by John Neilson and engraved by Peter Maverick [MSS 6552]

76: Interior photo of the Albert and Shirley Small Special Collections Library showing reference area. Photograph by Bryan Becker.

77: Interior photo of the Albert and Shirley Small Special Collections Library Small showing Albert H. Small Declaration of Independence gallery. Photograph by Bryan Becker.

78: Caesar Rodney, autograph letter signed to Thomas Rodney, 4 July 1776. [MSS 12568-a]

79: *In Congress, July 4, 1776, A Declaration by the Representatives of the United States of America, in General Congress Assembled* (New York, printed by Hugh Gaine, in Hanover Square, 1776) [KF 4506 .a1 1776d] • *In Congress, July 4, 1776, A Declaration by the Representatives of the United States of America, in General Congress Assembled* ([New York?, Samuel Loudon?, 1776]), 38 x 24 cm. [KF 4506 .A1 1776e]

80: Georgia fiscal document dated 6 December 1776 with signature of Button Gwinnett, speaker of the Georgia Assembly. [MSS 12569]

81: *Memorial of 100 Years as a Republic: Declaration of Independence* [Philadelphia: T.J. Berry, 1876], image 62 x 47 cm. on sheet 71 x 54 cm. [KF 4506 .A1 1865]

86: Photograph of Justice Sandra Day O'Connor, courtesy of AP Images, J. Scott Applewhite, photographer.

back cover:
Reenactment of fitting type for the printing of the John Dunlap broadside of the Declaration. Still image from *Declaring Independence* (see introductory note). • Albert H. Small. Photograph by Tom Cogill. • Reenactment of inspecting printed copy of the John Dunlap broadside of the Declaration. Still image from *Declaring Independence* (see introductory note).